How To A Business

JASON CROSS

Grant Thornton

KOGAN
PAGE

First published in 1992

Kogan Page Limited
120 Pentonville Road
London N1 9JN

British Library Cataloguing in Publication Data

A CIP record for this book is available from the British Library.

ISBN 0-7494-0583-X

Typeset by DP Photosetting, Aylesbury, Bucks
Printed and bound in Great Britain by
Biddles Ltd, Guildford and King's Lynn

Contents

Acknowledgements

Without the support of many colleagues and friends this book would not have been written. Some helped with ideas while others provided time to review drafts. Three people deserve special mention. David Fawcus provided a major contribution to the accuracy and completeness of Chapter 6 on taxation at a time when he was especially busy. Ron Pearson helped with the development of the checklist at the end of the book. Katie Forder spent many long hours converting my mumbled words or illegible script into readable drafts. To these people and all the others who helped, my thanks.

Jason Cross
December 1991

Introduction

How to Sell a Business is for the owners of both medium-sized and small businesses who are either considering selling their business, or those who believe that at some time in the future that may well be their wish and even those who do not wish to sell, since at any time they may receive an approach to sell or their circumstances might change.

The objective is to help business owners understand the selling process before they become involved in it. The book deals with the need to be clear as to what is being sold and why; the factors that can affect the selling price and possible ways of improving that price even when the timescale is limited; some of the more important tax implications of a business sale; the various sale methods; and the likely timescale involved and what help is available.

Most people only sell a business once. In doing so they are frequently selling their livelihood in exchange for a sum of money which will provide for their retirement. It is not the same as selling a house or a car: the process is much more complex and a thorough understanding of it can help to ensure that realistic objectives are set for the sale and all that is necessary is done to achieve these objectives.

Reasons for selling a business are varied. The book looks at many of these – some generated by a business's success, others by its failure. The potential unpleasantness of a forced sale can be alleviated by taking a logical course of action. By following the chapters in this book you should lessen the risk of a forced sale also being a bad sale.

This is not a technical manual. Indeed, given the range of unknown factors involved in selling a business, to write such a manual would be extremely difficult. Much of what is contained in this book is based upon experience and common sense; what may seem obvious is sometimes all too easily forgotten when negotiating the sale of a life's work. For example, the carrot of a higher price, which is paid over time, in return for the seller's continuing involvement in the business obviously contradicts a desire to retire immediately to the south of Spain, and therein lies the seed of future discontent. At worst this can develop into a full-scale clash with the purchaser which could precipitate the withholding of the additional cash expected. A more sensible sale would have been to have taken the lower figure immediately and achieved the set objective as planned.

Throughout the book there is an assumption that the reader has only a fairly basic knowledge of accounting and financial terminology. Many of the factors relating to a sale of the business may not be directly expressed in financial terms but ultimately, except in the most unusual cases, the process will lead to a sum of money passing from the buyer to the seller. A significant factor in determining the size of that sum will be the financial performance of the business and so accounting terms cannot be excluded. However, every attempt has been made to avoid unnecessary and confusing jargon.

A book is only a poor substitute for the benefits of sound advice from those with experience and expertise. Not only do the right advisers bring with them specific technical experience, but also, just as importantly, an objective perspective. They can help an owner to keep the emotional aspects of selling a business at bay, particularly during difficult price negotiations, by putting matters in context with other situations. Chapter 3 discusses what types of adviser may be the most suitable in particular situations and how to go about choosing them.

Tax legislation can have a material effect on the outcome of a sale of a business and especially on the amount of money that actually ends up in the seller's hands. Since such legislation and, often, its interpretation, is frequently changing, the most up-to-date advice should be sought. While every effort has been made to ensure that this book reflects tax legislation as it exists at the time of writing, by the time you read these words there will probably have been some changes.

1 *Why Are You Selling? And When?*

The reasons behind a decision to sell a business can be many, sometimes linked, sometimes coincidental for any particular sale. Just knowing that you want to sell is not really good enough. A seller needs to know as clearly as possible the exact reasons for sale so that when a sale package is finally agreed, the terms fit the maximum number of that seller's objectives. Only then are the sellers going to feel that they have had a good deal.

The first rule for the seller of a business is to be honest about the reasons for sale. Selling because of reaching retirement age may give rise to very different requirements from a sale than selling due to ill health. Not only might the actual requirements of the sale be different but also the steps taken to achieve a sale may need to be different, as may the timescale over which it will take place. A person suffering from ill health might become seriously distressed if it takes two years to prepare the business for sale in order to maximise the price, whereas somebody moving towards a natural retirement through age might well be much more willing to seek to maximise the potential price by such a delay.

Any emotional feelings must take second place to pragmatism, though this is difficult to do where a life's work is involved. An emotional approach to a sale can fudge the reasons for sale and the analysis of the objectives to be achieved, particularly price. At worst it can stop a sale altogether. Consulting experienced advisers from an early stage can ensure the necessary objectivity in setting the sale objectives.

Thus the reasons for a sale can affect timing. However, they may also have an effect on the price that can be obtained, who will be the possible buyers for the business and indeed, to whom the seller wants to sell. They may also affect the method of payment that will be acceptable to the seller.

Let us look at some of the most usual reasons for taking a decision to sell.

Retirement

One of the great advantages of owning a business is that in normal circumstances the owner can choose when to retire. Retirement here refers to what for most people is a decision linked with age: to slow down, reduce responsibilities and find much more time for activities away from work. A decision to sell for the purpose of retirement probably means turning a life's work into a pension fund. Therefore, great care should be taken in the planning of the sale. Most people have a reasonably clear idea of when they wish to retire which therefore allows plenty of planning time to maximise the returns on a sale.

One of the most important decisions that must be taken is whether the seller will be prepared to continue working in the business in some way after the sale if that is a requirement of the purchaser. Whether this will become an issue will depend on the nature of the business and the purchaser's ability to provide replacement management. If the purchaser does want the seller to stay for a time, refusal to do so may affect the selling price. This is an extremely personal decision dependent on the seller's own and his family's views. No one can give guidance as to which is the right decision but you will know which is right for you.

Selling because of impending retirement will usually allow adequate time to make the best sale possible and to deal with the many related tax matters. The best outcome is likely to be obtained by planning as far ahead as possible with a view to making a sale on a cyclical upswing in the economic or industry cycle, when the business is doing well and prices should be higher. But timing is tricky. Wait too long and suddenly the upswing has gone and prices are falling. Therefore, planned retirement is not a guarantee that the selling process will be easy and an optimum price obtained. External factors, such as interest rates and the state of the local or national economy, may move unexpectedly during the preparation period and cause a reduction in the price obtainable. But, in most cases early planning will result in a better outcome. This point is further elaborated in Chapter 6 when dealing with value of the business.

Ill health

If ill health is an important factor in the decision to sell, then, even if it is linked with reaching a natural retirement age, it could have important repercussions on the speed at which a sale should take place. Much will depend on the seriousness of the illness. If ill health is causing the owner to take his eyes off the running of the business then that in itself could cause the business to suffer. Small businesses are particularly vulnerable as they have little in the way of back-up management avilable. Under these circumstances the selling price obtainable will more than likely be reduced. Speed can then be extremely important in getting the best sale in such cases.

Ill health may also mean that any sale agreement ought not to include a requirement for the seller to continue in the business nor to receive part of the sale price by way of deferred payments.

There is a natural tendency for anyone owning a business to play down a health problem. Certainly, there is no reason for potential purchasers to be made aware of such a situation unnecessarily since clearly they will try to take advantage of it in any negotiation. However, long before reaching the negotiating stage it is important for the owner to face up to the situation so that the terms of the final sales agreement satisfy the most important needs of the seller. An unwillingness to do this may cause strain on both the seller and his family at a time when all should have been resolved and a comfortable retirement begun.

Diversification of investment

Most business people have two major assets: their house and their business. Unfortunately, in most cases the first often supports the financial backing for the second. In reality for many business people their sole investment is their business and if anything goes wrong with that then they may have little else left. Where a successful and saleable business has been built up there is a natural temptation to cash in so as not to be dependent in the future on one investment.

To illustrate, consider Mr Floyd who owns and runs an engineering business manufacturing metal boxes to order, primarily for the electrical contracting industry. On sales of £800,000 he makes a profit of £50,000 after paying himself £30,000. If Mr Floyd accepted an offer of £450,000 for the business not only could he invest that money and hope to receive an income of perhaps £25,000 per annum but he would also be released from liability for the overdraft of the business against which the bank is holding a mortgage on his house. Mr Floyd will receive a slightly lower income but without putting his house at risk.

Furthermore, the source of the income is now the result of investment in many companies, perhaps through a unit trust investment scheme, rather than being dependent solely on his own business. If diversification is the aim, an owner will have to be sanguine about the ongoing income level he can obtain if reinvestment is to be in quoted shares.

This is what diversification of investment means, put simply it involves a person moving away from having all his financial eggs in one basket. If this is indeed the prime motivation for a sale then there are a number of ways that this might be achieved other than by selling the whole of the business. Alternatives to outright sale will be discussed later in this chapter, some of which could be relevant in the above example.

Change of direction

Sometimes the owners of successful businesses decide that enough is enough and that they simply wish for a complete change in the direction of their lives. Who knows what the reasons for such decisions may be. One of the more frequent scenarios is the entrepreneur who has created a business from nothing, a business which has now reached stability and is therefore affected to a much greater extent by the economic environment than by the sheer willpower of the owner. Such a person can get bored and decide that it would be better to do something totally different. This may be to start up another business in a different, perhaps special interest, field, or even to search for that 'desert island', though experience shows they rarely stay there long. Frequently, the driving force behind this reason for sale is a loss of interest. Given that fact then such sales will normally be clean cut with no attempt to involve the owner beyond the sale date. In turn the seller will generally expect all payments for the business to be made at the time of sale with no allowance for any deferment thereof. After all the seller has no continuing commitment to the business and will not want to be in a position of risking part of his money at a time when all his attention is elsewhere.

Forced sale

Unfortunately, we all know that not every business is a success. If possible, it is as well to recognise this at an early stage so as to decide whether the business can be changed to make it successful or whether it would be best sold to someone else who could do more with it. If such decisions are delayed then the owner will be increasingly pressed to sell the business by those who are lending money to enable it to exist. In fact these lenders will be pushing to get their money back. In the first instance this may arise when the business is unable to make interest payments on monies that it has borrowed from its bank. From there it could be a slippery road to bankruptcy or liquidation.

If a sale is to some extent being forced upon the owner then, again, the length of time available for it to take place could well be foreshortened. Furthermore, if the business continues to deteriorate or lack performance it is probably in the best interest of all parties, including the owner, for such a sale to take place as soon as possible. Waiting, without making any changes, rarely ever saved a business. The term 'forced sale' means that the prime motivation for the sale is to repay monies due to other people with only a secondary requirement to leave as much in the hands of the owner as possible. Where there is the risk of losing everything including the owner's home if the business fails a speedy sale before the situation worsens may at least avoid that final traumatic experience. But speed does not mean planning is not possible.

An orderly sale is more likely to succeed than one carried out with little thought. In one case the owners of a particular company were being pressed by a lender to sell their business for about £100,000 to someone they had introduced. The business had been run badly, performance was poor and the owners were certainly not capable business people. A quick sale was indeed necessary. The owners thought the offer attractive since the proceeds would pay off the lender and release their house from the lender's security.

Before finally agreeing, the owners wisely sought professional advice. After half a day's analysis they were advised to advertise the business since there were likely to be a number of potential purchasers. This was not because the business was special, but because it had a workforce skilled in electronic assembly – something the adviser believed was in demand. Indeed within one week, a provisional offer of over £200,000 had been received and the lender held off until the transaction was completed. The owners, therefore, not only got their house back but after paying costs they banked £80,000.

An owner who was originally backed by friends or other family members who now wish to have their money back may be forced to sell. Because the company or business itself does not generate enough money to make such repayments, the owner may feel he has to sell it in order to meet the obligations entered into at the time he started. However, this might not be necessary. It may be possible to divide the business into several smaller units thereby enabling the sale of just part of the original business to raise the necessary cash. Or it may be sensible to raise new money in order to pay off the pressing lender. Certainly, no one should be forced to sell a successful business merely because it needs to repay monies at a certain point in time. There is nearly always another solution.

Changed market circumstances or technological changes may result in a forced sale. For example, a business which makes a large part of its sales to one customer is going to be faced with considerable difficulties if that customer states that they want to buy the business or they will take their contracts away. Alternatively, there is always a risk that such a dominant customer may say that they have become unhappy with the products and will take their custom elsewhere unless ownership changes.

This scenario can be very real in the case of businesses operating within the terms of franchise agreements. If the franchisor, that is the company giving out the franchise, decides that its franchised business is not being run properly they will frequently threaten to take the franchise away. They will require either that there are clear signs of improvement or that the business is sold to someone else with whom they are more satisfied. A classic example of this, although on a much larger scale, is the independent television contractor which fails to renew its contract. It is therefore eliminated from the business of broadcasting television programmes and is forced to sell that part of its business to another party. The obvious, and perhaps the only, buyer is the incoming contractor. If that contractor decides it does not want the assets then the outgoing contractor may have great difficulty in selling them. While such complications may seem a mile away from the average-sized business, similar situations do arise throughout the franchise industry.

Death or divorce

Death may give rise to a liability to pay inheritance tax. If the ownership of a business is the major asset, a sale may be necessary to raise sufficient funds to meet the tax liability. However, with the availability of significant reliefs and no tax payable in respect of smaller estates, many small businesses will avoid this problem. For larger businesses careful planning can mitigate the tax liability to a considerable extent. But a sudden unexpected death of an owner can cause the need for a sale.

In a divorce settlement where the principal asset is a business, there may be considerable pressure to sell. Even if the spouse is already a partial owner, it is normal for a buyer to be sought for that spouse's stake to avoid ongoing friction in the business.

In the case of both death and divorce, the time available to plan and organise a sale will normally be greater than on a business failure, enabling suitable steps to be taken to improve the potential proceeds. Furthermore in many cases a sale of the whole business may not be necessary. A partial sale may be possible thereby allowing the continuing owners to remain involved.

Bankruptcy or liquidation

Bankruptcy refers to businesses owned directly by the individual rather than through a company. A liquidation refers to a business set up as a company registered at Companies House. In either case the result is much the same. Someone else, the trustee in bankruptcy or the liquidator will take over responsibility for all the assets of the business and has an obligation to realise them as best he can in order to pay off the creditors of the business in a specified order. If the owner of a company has guaranteed certain liabilities of that company, frequently a bank overdraft, then he may find that he will also be at risk of going into bankruptcy in order to meet that guarantee, especially if he has risked all his assets in one investment. When an owner of a business should consider seeking the bankruptcy option and how a trustee in bankruptcy or a liquidator operates are outside the scope of this book and the sale of a business in these circumstances will not be referred to again.

Administration or receivership

In the case of a company which is in difficulty the directors may request the Court to appoint an Administrator. In most cases the Administrator will effectively take over the running of the business, with responsibility to the Court to put together a restructuring for the continuing existence of the business. In most cases this will result in the owners (ie shareholders) losing control of the business.

Similarly the appointment of an Administrative Receiver by holders of security over a company's assets – frequently the banks – will see the passing of control out of the owner's hands. The receiver has to raise sufficient funds to pay off those of the company's liabilities which by law he must. This he will generally achieve by either selling the business as a whole, one part of the business or assets of the business. Only if there is something left over will he return control to the shareholders. However, in most cases, the remaining creditors of the company – those who a receiver does not have to pay off – will exceed in value the returned assets and the company will go into liquidation.

Whether it be an administration or a receivership the owners have little effective control over sale. Therefore as for bankruptcy and liquidation, the sale of a business in these circumstances will not be discussed further.

Alternatives to sale

Depending on the reasons for sale, there are alternatives to achieving the desired end. The most usual alternatives to outright sale are partial sale, flotation, sale and leaseback of specific assets and share buy-ins.

Partial sale
If there is a desire to diversify investments but at the same time to retain an interest in the business then a partial sale is one route to consider. The first thing to be decided is whether you want to keep total control of the business and therefore to retain ownership of at least half or whether you would be prepared to allow somebody else to have control. Generally, it would only be in the latter circumstances that another business would look to purchase in what is termed a trade sale. Few ongoing businesses wish to have a minority stake in someone else's business. But that is certainly not the case with professional investors. These may be individuals who are interested in having a stake in other people's companies or various financial funds or institutions who specialise in buying minority stakes in private businesses. However, a sale of a minority stake to financial institutions or funds does normally

require that the business is in the form of a limited company. It is only in this way that the new minority investors feel that they have sufficient legal protection to leave the control of the business in another's hands.

Other ways of achieving partial sale include selling to interested members of the same family or selling a part to employees. If the latter is a realistic option, the price to be obtained can be expected to be lower; most employees will probably have only limited capital with which to buy a stake. However, it is possible to set up special funds or trusts to hold shares on behalf of employees both present and future. Dependent upon which type of arrangement is used it may also be possible for the employees to become direct holders of shares. This is a highly technical and complex area which if pursued further needs specialist advice.

The sale of a minority, or non-controlling, stake will not normally realise the same pro-rata price as a controlling stake. For example, if a business could be sold outright (ie. 100 per cent) for, say, £500,000, this might lead an owner to believe that a 30 per cent stake could be sold for £150,000. In reality it would probably realise less than half that sum, due to market demand, since there will be fewer people interested in purchasing a minority compared to a controlling stake.

Partial sale is a particularly good alternative where cash is required because of death or divorce. However, any minority investor will seek to satisfy himself that neither event has weakened the business's potential to grow and succeed.

Flotation

In times of economic boom there may be many owners of businesses who wish to see the shares of their company sold through the Stock Exchange. Obtaining a flotation on the Stock Exchange is a difficult process but if ultimately achieved it may well include a partial sale of the owner's shares to other people through the Stock Exchange. But here we are talking about fairly large companies with a strong growth record, a full management team and profits running at a level of at least £1m per annum. Even this level of profits will probably only gain acceptance for the company to the second-tier market, known as the Unlisted Securities Market. As this process is not generally open to the smaller business it will only be referred to briefly again in Chapter 3 when dealing with the question of advisers.

Sale and leaseback

Sale and leaseback refers to the mechanism whereby a business can sell some of its business assets, generally land and buildings or major items of plant, to a third party for cash. The third party then leases the property or equipment back to the business under specific arrangements for payment of rent and period of lease. While this is a recognised way for businesses to raise money directly it can also be used as a means of raising money for owners without selling a business. It is particularly relevant in cases where:

1. the business is not a limited company and thus legally the assets are owned directly by the owner of the business;
2. the business is a limited company but the land and buildings from which it operates are owned directly by the owners of the business rather than through the company. To have real value for a sale this property will need to be either freehold or held on a long leasehold.

Although this type of transaction generally relates to land and buildings, it is possible to achieve the same thing with particularly good quality plant and equipment, such as printing machines. In carrying out this transaction there are, of course, two sides to the deal. The buyer is generally only undertaking to purchase the asset on the basis that in leasing it back to the business he is going to get paid the required rentals when they are due in the future. Thus, the buyer's decision whether or not to enter into such a transaction will depend upon the creditworthiness of the business which is selling, not because it is a seller, but because it is leasing the asset back. Furthermore, in dealing with land and buildings the important criteria as to location and use, which any buyer who is then going to lease out the property will set, will need to be satisfied. In the case of plant and equipment the creditworthiness of the company is even more important because the last thing that the new owner wants is to be forced to take the equipment back and sell it again.

As with most transactions, there are important tax implications in a sale and leaseback and thought must be given to these at an early stage to avoid risk of failing to achieve the objective.

Share buy-in

Under the Companies Act 1985 it is possible in the UK for companies to buy back their own shares from the shareholders and pay for them in cash held by the company. Therefore, it is possible to obtain cash payment from a company without actually changing its ownership. Whether a company can actually carry out such a buy-in depends on whether it meets certain specified criteria at the time. If it does then the process for doing this has to be followed carefully and the tax implications fully appreciated. In many cases there will be a simpler method of achieving the same result.

Dividend payment

One of those simpler methods is to pay a substantial dividend out of the company. As with a share buy-in this does assume that the company has the cash available or can raise sufficient cash to make such a payment. The particular disadvantage of this option is that the dividend is income and if the payment is large enough it will be subject to income tax at the highest rates. However, this may be better than leaving surplus cash in a company whose fortunes could change. In the meantime any cash extracted can be invested elsewhere. But as with any extraction of cash from a business it is important to ensure that sufficient cash is left within the business to enable it to flourish.

Timing of an outright sale

On the assumption that outright sale remains the chosen option, now is the point at which to consider how long the sale process might take. The aim as regards timing for sale must be, as far as possible, to sell when demand for the relevant type of business is high and the performance of the business is at its best. Unfortunately, it is hard to make the two patterns come together at the right moment. There will always be an element of luck in the timing of the sale. But by giving careful thought to the real reasons for sale, an accurate assessment of the state of the business and what can be done in the time available it is possible to increase the chances of a successful sale.

The question of grooming the business for sale is discussed later in Chapter 4. Certain steps can be taken to make sure the business is looking its best at the time of sale and that market conditions for a sale are at or near the optimum. However, in many cases it is not practical to take so long and at the other extreme, a forced sale will require immediate action even when market conditions are bad.

2 *What Are You Selling?*

There are a number of ways in which one can own part or all of a business. The three terms which are best known are 'sole trader', 'partnership' and 'limited company'. Frequently, the term 'company' is used to mean the same thing as the word 'business' but within the context of this book it is used to refer to a limited liability company. The term 'business' is used to refer to any form of business structure.

Sole trader

To illustrate the differences of the above three terms, consider the business history of Mr Geoffrey. After some years working as a site manager for a large firm of electrical contractors Mr Geoffrey decided to set up his own business. He believed he had found a gap in the market whereby he arranged to provide contracting services for the refurbishment of blocks of flats at considerably less cost than the larger companies. Time proved him to be right and after two years he was employing five other people. At that stage his business, called Geoffrey's Contractors, operated as a sole trader. Mr Geoffrey owned all the assets of the business himself and all the creditors of the business had a claim against him personally. There was no distinction in law between his personal assets, such as his house and his furniture, and his business assets.

Partnership

At this point Mr Geoffrey agreed to join forces with another contractor in a similar line of business called Davis Contractors. Mr Geoffrey and Mr Davis agreed to change the name of the combined business to G & D Contractors and enter into a partnership agreement. In this particular partnership agreement, Mr Geoffrey and Mr Davis decided that the share in the business should be 60 per cent to Mr Geoffrey and 40 per cent to Mr Davis, reflecting the relevant sizes of the two original businesses. G & D Contractors was now a partnership.

What does partnership mean as regards the ownership of the assets? In general terms, every asset of the business now had two owners and every person who was owed money by the business had two partners against whose assets they could seek recompense, whether those assets were business assets or personal assets. In English law a partnership as such cannot enter into a contract. It is the individual partners who take on the contractual obligations. In Scotland this is slightly different since under Scottish law there is recognition of a partnership as being a separate legal entity, but the ultimate responsibility of the partners for the business liabilities is effectively the same.

Limited company

After a further two years the business of G & D Contractors had grown significantly and included electrical refurbishing of offices and commercial premises as well as flats. In order to expand further Mr Geoffrey and Mr Davis needed to take in a financial partner. In particular, they needed a cash injection to expand the business's storage area and office space. For a variety of reasons, which are not relevant here, the two partners were advised that the time had come to convert their partnership into a limited liability company. This is a legal structure which under both English and Scottish law has a separate entity from the people who own it. Thus from that point the new G & D Contractors Limited, which bought the old partnership business in exchange for shares in the new company, contracted with its suppliers and customers in its own name. The individual partners became shareholders in the company and were no longer personally responsible for the liabilities of the company other than in those cases where they had to give personal guarantees in respect of amounts due. From then on Mr Geoffrey and Mr Davis could take in new business partners by arranging for the company to issue shares in exchange for cash.

Mr Geoffrey's small business developed from being a sole trader to a limited liability company. When it comes to selling a business it is necessary to be clear as to what its structure is. In the case of a limited company the shareholders will be entering into a contract to sell their shares while in the case of a sole trader or a partnership the owner or partners will be entering into personal contracts to sell the assets of the business. In the case of a company the liabilities of the business will pass with that business, whereas in the case of a sole trader or partnership they will remain the liabilities of the owners. When considering the subject of the asking price (Chapter 6) it will be clear why it is important from the outset to be aware of the nature or legal structure of the business one is selling.

Business assets

Whatever the legal structure of the business a sale will include the business assets. These will generally consist of the property in which the business is based, whether freehold or leasehold, manufacturing plant and equipment if it is a manufacturing business, shop fittings if it is a retail business, office equipment and furniture and if relevant, motor vehicles. All these assets are generally referred to as *fixed assets*. Then there are the *current assets*, the most usual of which are stocks, work-in-progress and finished goods and debtors. Sometimes you may hear the phrase *tangible assets* used to refer to both fixed and current assets together.

But a business is not only made up of physical assets that you can touch or of monies that are due to the business. There are also *intangible assets*. The business may manufacture goods which are dependent upon the right to someone's invention. This invention will be protected by a patent and the business should have negotiated rights to manufacture within the patent. That particular right to manufacture may have considerable value. Similarly, a right to publish certain written material or to use certain trade marks can have value and they are just as much an asset to the business as a motor car. Another example is a mailing list. If a mailing list has been put together to serve a particular purpose and therefore aimed at a specific group of people, then that list may well have a significant value to another business also trying to target that same group of people, possibly with a different product.

The best known intangible asset is frequently referred to as *goodwill*. The value of goodwill in a business is looked at by the owners as being the value of having contracts, a customer base and a sound reputation in the market place. The better known the name the greater the importance of the goodwill to a buyer may be.

Asset-based and people-based businesses

In looking at what one has to sell it is as well to think about the nature of the business. The most common distinction is that made between an asset-based business and a people-based business. At one extreme you will have a property investment business, that is a business which buys properties to rent out to third parties. This is clearly an asset-based business. It is heavily dependent on the ability to buy property at a value which will allow it to receive rent which will cover the cost of borrowing money to make the original purchase. In such a business you may have investment properties that were purchased for £500,000 on which there is an income after expenses and payments of interest on monies borrowed of, say, £20,000.

Compare that with a people-based business. Such businesses are generally service industry and extremely dependent on certain individuals. For example, an advertising agency will be heavily dependent upon the creative ability of its people since it is creativity which will generally entice clients to spend their money. The physical assets of such a business may be no more than a short-term, rented office, which has little value, and office equipment. In this case you could have a business with assets of say £20,000 also generating an income after expenses of £20,000.

Though the two businesses may make the same profit, when it comes to the price that may be obtainable, it will differ considerably. The people-based business is almost totally dependent on the continuing co-operation of the people. If there is discontent, then the assets (the people) can leave. The risks of purchase are therefore greater and the price will generally be lower. Property assets may lose value in a recession but they cannot walk out on you and this will be reflected in the price. Hence, it is as well to know from the outset to what extent the business you are selling is an asset-based or a people-based business.

Franchises

A growing number of small and medium-sized businesses in the UK are termed franchises. In essence these are businesses run along predetermined lines, those lines being set out by either the manufacturer of the goods that are supplied to the franchise (such as motor cars) or by the originator of a format which has proved to be successful in the market place (such as fast-food outlets). Agreements between franchisors and franchisees vary from franchise to franchise, but in most cases there will be constraints upon the ability of the franchisee to sell. All such sales will be subject to prior agreement by the franchisor who will be concerned that the purchaser can fulfil the requirements and the standards set down. Franchise agreements are rarely transferable to a third party, even with the agreement of the franchisor. What generally happens is that the buyer will buy the assets of the outgoing franchisee and will then enter into a new franchise agreement with the franchisor. The franchisor therefore effectively controls the whole transaction and can have a major influence on the price that is paid to the seller. Despite this control a good franchisor will be keen to see that the franchisee gets a fair price for the business otherwise they will lose the confidence of the other franchisees who may want to sell their businesses sometime in the future. If, however, the outgoing franchisee has not performed well then the franchisor may not be particularly concerned what price they get and may not be particularly co-operative.

One of the advantages of being a seller or a buyer of a franchise is that there is generally plenty of information available on the performance of the business. This helps to make assessment of the right value for the business much easier. The information will enable a buyer to check how a particular operation compares with other operations within the franchise network generally. This can help a buyer to make up his mind and therefore achieve a sale more quickly.

Key factors

In deciding what you have to sell it is also worth bearing in mind the key factors which may attract someone to buy the business in the first place. These will naturally vary from one type of business to another and from one individual to another. A few at least are likely to be of importance whatever the deal.

- Is the business profitable?
- Are the profits improving from year to year?
- Does the business generate cash or does it require cash to be injected in order to expand?
- Are the assets of good quality?

- Are they well maintained?
- Is the location of the business suitable?
- Is there a good customer base?
- Is the market for the business's products expanding or declining?
- If the business is in the retail trade is there a suitable catchment area?
- Has the business had difficulties obtaining either the goods or people it needs?
- Are arrangements with suppliers stable?
- Does the business depend on one or two individuals, including the owner, for its survival?
- Are there good financial records in existence and can the financial information be supported if the buyer wants to carry out an investigation?

These are just a few of the questions that a potential buyer will seek to answer. It is as well for the seller to consider them at an early stage since they help to highlight for him what is to be sold.

3   Professional Advisers

For most owners selling their business is a major event in their lives. It is usually less frequent than selling a house, which itself requires the assistance of at least two professional advisers; an estate agent who will advise on the asking price for the property and organise the marketing of the property, and a lawyer who will advise on the various legal requirements in order to make the sale a success. The selling of a business tends to be rather more complicated. As a result there are numerous types of adviser who might be considered. This chapter looks at who those advisers might be and some of the ways to choose them.

But first, a warning; choose the right level of advice for the particular sale being carried out. It is no use expecting to employ a merchant bank to market a business and sell it if that business is a restaurant with a turnover of £200,000. Merchant banks are not geared to handle that size of business and would not add the right sort of value to make the transaction more successful for the seller. If the choice is made correctly then the fees that are charged by the advisers will be well worthwhile. The advisers should not only have helped to obtain the best price but also structured the transaction in such a way as to bring peace of mind to the seller.

Apart from fees, there are two critical factors to be taken into account when choosing advisers.

1. Does the adviser concerned have the right sort of experience? The seller should find out what the adviser has done before and what similar businesses he has been involved in selling, so that he can get a feel for his competence.
2. Does the adviser inspire confidence? Going through a sale transaction can be a traumatic experience and a seller must feel he can rely fully on his advisers throughout. It is extremely difficult and expensive to change advisers half-way through a transaction.

The seller should not hesitate to see a number of different advisers in the category that he wants. But before making any choice careful thought must be given to which type of advisers are needed. A discussion of some of the possibilities follows.

Lawyers

Without doubt the seller will need to employ a legal adviser. When selling a business there is almost certainly going to be a *sale and purchase* agreement. That agreement needs to set down in legal form who is selling and who is buying, what is being sold, the timing of the sale, the price that is going to be paid and the method of payment. This agreement needs to be drafted in clear terms so that misunderstandings can be avoided. The last thing that any seller or purchaser requires is to enter into a subsequent dispute that may end up in a court of law. It is important therefore to have on board a lawyer who has carried out this type of work before. A lawyer who is used to doing divorce work or even property conveyencing may not necessarily be suited to advising on the legal aspects of selling a business.

Most business owners, at some stage during their business career, will have had need of a lawyer. Probably that lawyer will be a good business lawyer with the right sort of experience to help him, but not necessarily. Some of the matters on which legal advice has been sought in the past may not be relevant to the experience that is now needed. So a seller should talk openly with his lawyer, if he already has one, to make sure that he really does have the required experience. One of the principal distinctions that will need to be made is whether assets are being sold or a limited company. If it is the latter, then the contents of the sale and purchase agreement will be different from one relating to a sale and purchase of assets. Thus the lawyer needs to be one well versed in company law.

Accountants

Most businesses employ outside accountants for one reason or another. For small businesses that may be to write up the actual accounting records or to draw up annual figures for the purposes of completing returns to the Inland Revenue. Others may use accountants to draw up figures to raise money from the bank. If the business concerned is a limited company then there will certainly be auditors to that company and they will be accountants. Even if not a company, many businesses will still call upon their accountants to perform some level of audit. Therefore, just as for lawyers, the business owner will generally already have accountants 'on board'.

The same questions relating to experience should be asked of the accountants as of the lawyers. Preparing figures for submission to the Inland Revenue or carrying out an audit on a small company does not provide the necessary experience for advising on the sale of a business. On a sale an accountant adviser should have experience of how to show the numbers in their best light, how to value the business and how to bring out the favourable features during the course of negotiation. As the transaction proceeds the accountant will inevitably get involved in producing a series of figures to explain to the potential purchaser the performance of the business, its assets and its liabilities. As the transaction draws to a conclusion the accountant's role becomes especially important since it will be he who helps to draw up the final set of numbers as of the date of the sale. If the sale involves some payments on future dates then the seller will again need the accountant if those payments are dependent upon the subsequent performance of the business.

Tax advisers

In smaller transactions advice needed in respect of tax may not be complex and will relate primarily to the personal taxation of the sellers. In particular, advice will be needed to ensure maximum availability of reliefs, especially from capital gains tax. In larger transactions the complications can be much more significant because the structure of the transaction will have to reflect as far as possible both the requirements of the seller and of the purchaser. Whatever the circumstances tax advice will be needed.

In most cases the principal tax advisers will be the accountants who are helping the seller. However, such advice can also be given by lawyers if they have the in-house expertise. To avoid duplication of effort, and therefore the possible duplication of fees, the seller should make it clear from the outset how he wishes his accountants or his lawyers to work together on tax matters.

Valuers

If land and buildings are involved in the sale it may be advisable to obtain valuations of that property to make sure that it is fully reflected in the asking price. However, this may not always be the case. When selling a petrol station on a small country road the value of the site is probably almost totally dependent on the volume of petrol and oil that is sold through the site. This will be determined to a significant extent by the traffic flow on that road. Thus as a garage site there may be no benefit in obtaining an outside valuation. However, that valuation may be of benefit if in fact the site has an alternative use to which it could be put and which might make it more valuable than using it as a garage. If that was indeed the case, then in effect one would be selling not a garage business but a piece of land.

In a few cases the planning consent relating to the land may be critical. A garage site has consent for fuel storage. Such consent can be difficult to obtain near built-up areas. So even if it was a low volume site it may have significant value where there is a new development planned involving fuel storage.

Clearly in a forced sale the best that one may be able to obtain for the business is the value of the assets. In such cases for a manufacturing business it may be worthwhile to have valuations of machinery and equipment. There are specialist valuers well versed in this type of valuation. However, machinery that is highly specialised and only relevant to a particular business may be severely restricted in value.

Patent agents

If, as part of the business, the company or the owner holds patents at some stage the owner will have employed the services of a patent agent. This is really a specialist lawyer who deals with all aspects of patents, as well as such matters as trade marks. A patent agent will not only advise on the strength of a patent but will also assist you to maintain the enforceability of the patent. If patents and/or trade marks are part of the business being sold then the purchaser will undoubtedly use his own patent agent to investigate their strength. The seller may then have a need for his own patent agent to help handle questions raised and in the negotiations.

Actuaries

These days, it is not unusual for even medium-sized businesses to have their own pension schemes. Such a scheme will be funded by the contributions from the company and, probably, from the employees. When a sale of the business takes place the workforce is likely to be one of the principal assets of the business and therefore it is important that their terms of employment, which will include their pension arrangements, are not changed for the worse. Making sure that the ongoing pension arrangements are satisfactory is important.

From the seller's point of view it is necessary to determine whether or not the pension fund has adequate resources to meet the potential liabilities on it. This will be determined by an actuary who is a specialist in this field. More often than not he will find that either the pension fund is over-funded, that is where the funds within the pension fund are deemed to be more than is necessary to meet the potential liabilities, or conversely that it is under-funded. If the fund is over-funded then a purchaser of the business could determine that future payments to the fund would be less than would otherwise be the case. The purchaser will therefore gain a financial advantage. It is as well for the seller to be aware of this so that a better price can be negotiated from the purchaser.

Conversely if the pension fund is under-funded the purchaser may well require that the seller makes up the difference by making an additional payment to the fund. Alternatively, the purchaser may undertake to do so himself but only on the basis that the price paid for the business is reduced by a similar amount.

Most types of valuation require the making of important assumptions. Thus two valuers frequently arrive at two different values. Actuaries are no different. Therefore, as in these circumstances, the purchaser is likely to have an actuary advising, the seller will also need to employ one. However, if the business does not have its own pension fund but merely contributes to the state pension scheme it is most unlikely that the seller will need to employ an actuary.

Merger and acquisition boutiques and business transfer agents

Over recent years there have grown up a significant number of *corporate finance boutiques*. One of the services they provide is to take on mandates for the sale of a business. In effect they are agreeing to advise the sellers on all aspects of the sale of their business, to market that business and to help structure a deal. A merger and acquisition boutique is more of a facilitator, putting into place the various aspects of a deal needed to make a transaction successful. Most offer experienced advice but some are indistinguishable from *business transfer agents* who are primarily in the business of finding a buyer for the business rather than advising. Their interest is to make sure the transaction actually happens. They can have an important role but it is necessary to be clear whether one is seeking an adviser or a broker. That does not mean to say that business transfer agents do not take great care over their reputations. They realise that these would be severely tarnished if they did not take proper account of the owner's requirements.

In the realm of business advice generally it can be extremely difficult to make distinctions between one category of adviser and another. The services carried out by a merger and acquisition boutique are also carried out by many accountants and to some extent by a number of lawyers. It is worth bearing in mind that if merger and acquisition boutiques are used there will almost certainly still be a need to employ a lawyer and an accountant as well.

Merchant banks

Most merchant banks have merger and acquisition departments. These teams operate as advisers to either buyers or sellers in much the same way as the merger and acquisition boutiques but they are generally on the look out for larger transactions. It is unlikely that a transaction with a value of less than £5m will be of much interest to them and that minimum level will be a lot higher for the larger merchant banks. However, if flotation is being considered as an alternative to a sale, then seeking the advice of a merchant bank may well be necessary.

The above is a list of some of the more usual advisers that may be needed when selling a business. However, it is worth remembering that there are many overlaps between the activities of advisers. Many accountancy firms will accept mandates to help find a buyer for a business. In finding that buyer their activities will be little different from those of a merger and acquisition boutique or a merchant bank. One significant difference, however, is that they will have in-house accounting and tax advice. Legal firms have their own network of contacts to enable them to find potential buyers for a business. Similarly, both lawyers and accountants do provide tax advice. For the smaller business it is probably best to choose first either the business's solicitor or accountant and then to develop the relationship with other advisers if and when necessary. In this way the seller will be able to avoid duplication of fees more easily.

Fees

It is a fact of business life that advisers have to be paid. However, when selling a business it is also extremely difficult to say how much they are likely to cost. Total fees will depend on the size of the transaction, the nature and quality of the business being sold, the requirements for active marketing and the complication of the agreed transaction. If advisers are chosen with care, so that their expertise is truly relevant to the particular situation, a seller should obtain full value, both by receiving a better price and achieving peace of mind.

When taking on any form of adviser the seller should agree in writing exactly what he wants that adviser to do. This is generally called a 'letter of engagement'. The more detailed this letter is the easier it will be to avoid arguments over whether or not certain fees are properly payable. One section of the letter should clearly state in what circumstances fees are payable and how they are calculated, both if the sale proceeds successfully and if it is aborted.

Fees are closely associated with the market for the services at that time. It is therefore difficult to be precise about what to expect because, by the time you read this book, the market situation may be very different from that at the time of writing. But there are a few general pointers that can be given.

First, whoever is appointed as the principal adviser on how to market the business and actually to carry out the sale will probably be prepared to be paid at least partly on a success fee basis. If no sale takes place, because a buyer cannot be found, then a fee may not have to be paid at all, or perhaps only a minimum payment to cover the preparation and production of marketing documents. Whatever the fee arrangements, they should be set out in the letter of engagement which should specify when fees are payable, how they are to be calculated and when payment is to be made.

Second, a common area of dispute over fees is whether the

buyer was or was not introduced by the adviser. Most advisers providing this service require an exclusive agreement for a minimum specified period of time. This means that unless agreed otherwise, fees will be payable to the adviser even if the business is sold to someone or some company known previously to the owner. Thus, the letter of engagement should also detail when a fee will not be payable as well as what happens if the owner decides not to sell after all. If the latter is the case the owner must expect to pay some fees for the work done by the adviser up to the time of the change of mind, and it is as well to specify up front what this fee will be.

Third, in general the services of lawyers and accountants are paid for on a time-related basis. Clearly, anyone who is paid for giving advice, including accountants and lawyers, is putting him or herself at some risk should that advice prove to be wrong. The level of their fee will therefore reflect that risk but even so it is usually true that the longer a transaction takes the more expensive it will be. For this reason it is difficult to get fixed quotations from lawyers or accountants unless it is an unusually straightforward transaction. All that is likely to be given is an indicator of cost and so it is as well to explore whether or not it is a fee based on everything going right first time or a rather more practical estimate. Even though fees may be based, or more strictly, related to the time involved, a basis which involves a lower rate of fees if the transaction does not proceed but a higher rate if it does may be negotiated.

Though it must be emphasised that there is no standard method of calculating the likely level of fees, the following is just one example of what can actually happen.

Mr X approached a well-known firm of accountants to advise him on the sale of his company. After initial discussions it was agreed that they would help Mr X find a buyer, act as his financial adviser throughout the transaction and provide tax advice in respect of the transaction. The fees were structured as follows:

1. The sum of £2,500 for preparing a sales memorandum.
2. Three per cent of gross sale proceeds up to £600,000 plus 5 per cent on proceeds in excess of that amount. The £2,500 fee above would be set against this fee.
3. Fees for taxation advice to be based on time spent.

The £600,000 figure mentioned was a realistic assessment of the likely sale price of the company. If a sale did not take place Mr X's exposure to fees was limited to £2,500 plus any time spent on tax advice.

In the event an offer of £750,000 was received and a sale completed at that price. Total professional fees paid were £25,500 for financial advice, nearly £4,000 for tax advice and just over £11,000 for legal fees (all amounts quoted exclude value added tax). This represented about 5 per cent of the sale price, which itself was higher than expected.

4 *Preparation For Sale*

Once a decision has been taken to sell a business there are a number of steps that may be taken to improve the price that may be obtained. This is frequently referred to as 'grooming the business for sale'. Some of the steps are real, others tend to be presentational. What can actually be done will depend on the nature of the business, how it has been run and financed in the past and the time available before the business is put up for sale.

Profits

For many businesses, though not all, one of the most important factors in determining its value to a buyer is the level of profits generated. Thus, if time allows, profits should be groomed from as early a stage as possible. If the business is being run on an extremely tight basis already then it may be that little can in fact be done. However, in the case of most family run or controlled businesses there can be many reasons why it has not been run in a way that necessarily produces maximum profits. It is not intended to offer a lengthy section on how to improve the profits of a business generally. That is a wide subject and warrants an entire book in its own right. However, the following few suggestions, if relevant, will produce an improved profit line prior to sale. First consider why there is a need to show, if possible, an improvement in the profits.

A business that is valued essentially on the basis of its profits will be valued on a multiple of those profits (see Chapter 6). Higher profits, even though taxable, should lead to a considerably higher price being obtained. For a business that may be valued on five times its annual profits a £100 increase in profits now will put £500 on the price. The possible penalty is that the increase of £100 may be subject to tax. However, that is a small price to pay for the increased price obtainable within quite a short space of time.

Discretionary expenditure

The principal area to look at is *discretionary expenditure*, that is expenditure not absolutely necessary to keep the business going. In a family business one of the most usual areas where expenditure may be unnecessarily incurred beyond that really needed for the good of the business is in travel and entertainment. For example expensive overseas business trips. It is not surprising that this occurs since, if the owner of the business does have to make overseas trips, then why not do it comfortably rather than on a shoe string, which would increase profits and tax payable? The same goes for entertaining expenditure, though this is not an allowable business charge for tax purposes.

There is also the question of employing one's family in jobs which are not fully necessary for the business. Spouses are often employed in the business in a small way so that they can earn sufficient to benefit from their personal tax allowances. Of course, they may actually be doing a job for which they should be paid three times as much but that is not the most usual scenario. In this particular piece of grooming it may not be necessary to 'sack the other half' but rather to isolate the cost so it can be highlighted when preparing figures for a possible buyer. Similarly, family members or shareholders may be paid amounts considerably in excess of that payable to professional managers for the same job. This excess directors' remuneration should also be highlighted.

Motor car expenses frequently contain a discretionary element. There are good reasons why an owner of a business may wish to run an extremely expensive car on the business; it would almost certainly be cheaper than trying to run it himself. However, is it really necessary to run a Rolls–Royce as opposed to a Vauxhall Senator? The additional expense so incurred is one that could be saved and is truly discretionary.

In a similar way, what about that office in the south of Spain (or is it a villa)? Is it really necessary to have an aircraft or helicopter for the business with all the attendant costs? And then there is that sponsorship of the owner's favourite sport. To owners of smaller businesses, such questions may seem totally out of order given that they could never afford to involve themselves in such expenditure. However, this is not always the case with some of the more highly successful medium-sized businesses (and regrettably some that are not so successful!).

Rather than actually eliminating discretionary expenditure, details of it can be highlighted when providing information to a potential buyer, but it is harder to establish the amount of the potential saving than to achieve it. Therefore if a good time is available within which to prepare a business for sale, it could be wise to sacrifice the Rolls–Royce in exchange for a little less comfort now and a higher price for the business at the end of the day.

Cost reduction

There may be some areas of expenditure which are less discretionary but could be pruned all the same. During the run up to actual sale, is all the planned maintenance to the building truly necessary? Can the resurfacing of the car park be put off? Can the replacement of office furniture be slowed down? Is it important to have new flags for the flagpoles? Depending on the nature of the business, there may well be many similar questions that should be asked.

However, be warned. It is important not to cut back expenditure which is necessary to maintain the core level of profits of the business. Thus cutting back on replacing machinery or on its maintenance may actually reduce the price obtainable unless there has in fact been a trend of excessive expenditure in this area in the past. There is no point in reducing marketing and advertising expenditure if it is actually going to cause your level of sales to drop and it would be unwise to delay replacement of vehicles which continually break down on the motorway and so cost large sums for recovery. A well-advised purchaser of the business will look at expenditure trends and if a fall in core areas of expenditure is noted then explanations are going to be sought as to whether such reductions were actual reductions in excessive expenditure or actually in core expenditure. Thus, a seller needs to keep a balanced view on how the profits are improved in this way.

Accounting policies

So far cutting expenditure which causes money actually to go out of the door has been considered, but there are other ways whereby profits may be shown to be, in reality, better than previously disclosed. In particular this may be in the area of making provisions against the value of stock, whether it be raw materials or finished goods, against losses or potential losses on contracts that may have been undertaken, and against the possibility of bad debts. If over the years provisions have been made in the accounts against the possibility of these losses then it could be that the disclosure of both the profits and the assets of the business are lower than they really are. Consideration should be given to reviewing these arrangements to see whether it would be beneficial to change them. However, there can be important tax implications in taking any such decisions and relevant professional advice should be sought before carrying out any changes in the business's provisions policy.

A further area of accounting policies which can affect disclosed profits is that relating to the depreciation of assets. If trailers are depreciated over three years when in reality they last ten years or more, the effect is to understate profits. Conversely, if tractor units are depreciated over ten years when they rarely last more than five, then the effect on profit is the reverse.

The following example looks at the effect some of these changes can have on profit. Mr Harding and his wife have accounts for the last year showing a profit of £15,000. This is profit available to be paid by way of dividend out of their company and is after charging a proper salary for Mr Harding and a £4,000 salary for Mrs Harding, whose sole role has been to provide catering at occasional marketing events. Mr Harding drives a Rolls–Royce owned by the company while Mrs Harding drives a VW Golf GTI, also owned by the company. Mr Harding takes an overseas trip each year to the Far East to visit his agents. This trip costs £7,500 as Mr Harding travels first class, stays in the top hotels and entertains extensively. A further business trip is taken each winter to Brazil. This is also to meet the company's agent but on this trip Mr Harding is accompanied by his wife who was born in Brazil. This trip costs £11,000. In incurring this expenditure Mr Harding is not doing anything wrong. He and the company duly disclose the expenditure to the Inland Revenue who make such adjustments as are agreed both to the company's and to Mr and Mrs Harding's individual tax assessments. Cash flow is not affected either and the company always pays its creditors on time. What we are looking at is the question of eliminating some of this discretionary expenditure in order to boost profits and therefore the price that a buyer will pay. Mr Harding knows that the business could run just as effectively without his wife being involved; £10,000 a year could be saved if he drove a less expensive car; a further £2,500 could be saved on his trip to the Far East without affecting the level of business he does and the trip to Brazil could be eliminated, since the amount of business done with Brazil is small and unprofitable. The savings per year could look like this:

		£
Replacing Rolls–Royce with another car		10,000
Saving on travel to Far East		2,500
Eliminating travel to Brazil		11,000
Not employing Mrs Harding – salary		4,000
– car		4,000
	Total saving	£31,500

It can be seen that if the above items were saved the profit of Mr and Mrs Harding's company would be shown as £46,500, a much more impressive figure for a potential buyer. The extent to which such savings can actually be demonstrated in the preparation period before sale will depend on the time available. Indeed, it may be that some of the savings will not actually be made but sufficient information will be maintained to demonstrate the amount of this discretionary expenditure to a potential buyer.

Working capital

Working capital refers to the amount of money that a business needs to cover its current assets, such as stocks of raw materials and finished products, the value of work-in-progress and the financing of the debtors due to the company. Against this figure would be offset *current liabilities*, that is the amounts of money due to people for services, goods, wages, tax, etc. In many businesses the money required for working capital is supplied by way of overdraft from the bank if it is not provided by the owners themselves. The working capital in Mr and Mrs Harding's company can be summarised as follows:

	£
Stock of finished goods	100,000
Debtors	150,000
	250,000
Amounts due to suppliers	(60,000)
PAYE due	(5,000)
Corporation tax due	(10,000)
Working capital required	£175,000

At first sight it might appear that having current assets that are over three times higher than current liabilities is a positive situation from the point of view of a potential buyer. However, that £175,000 has to be financed from somewhere. In the case of Mr Harding's company, it is all financed from overdraft on which, of course, the company is paying interest. At 12 per cent that is an additional cost to the business of £21,000. So what could be done about this to improve profitability?

The first step is to determine whether the level of stock held by the business is larger than necessary. The ability to do this will depend on the nature of business. Some businesses have long order cycles. Most are not large enough to be able to demand of suppliers that they deliver at short notice. But experience shows that stock is frequently carried at too high a level by many businesses, large and small.

Next, there is the question of how long customers are allowed to take to pay. In many businesses the standard terms for payment are 30 days from invoice date. Yet outstanding debts may reflect a value equivalent to two or three months' sales. Every pound collected earlier is one pound less requirement for working capital. In the case of Mr Harding's company it is estimated that some £40,000 could be cut out of the working capital requirement by improving the efficiency of both the stock holding and the recovery of monies due from customers.

In some cases it may be possible to improve the working capital position by making better use of one's creditors. An ideal situation is not to have to pay suppliers until the goods they have supplied have been sold and the cash received for them. It is in this way, for example, that some food retailers have financed their stocks. For most businesses this ideal is beyond reach but there is no reason not to take all the credit that is available from suppliers. Not to do so is increasing the costs of the business and reducing its profit. In looking at Mr and Mrs Harding's company it is found that it is an over prompt payer both of government, local government and supplier debts. It is estimated that it could reduce its overdraft by a further £40,000 if it used all the credit that was available to it. In a full year the interest saving at 12 per cent on this total working capital reduction of £80,000 would increase profits by £9,600, a considerable sum when compared with the original profit figure of £15,000.

It might be argued that an incoming buyer would see the possibilities for savings in working capital when looking at the business and would therefore make allowances for this in the price that he offered. However, though that might be the case – and it might be one of the incentives for a buyer to buy – the argument for an increased price will hold much greater force when the savings are actually being made and profit enhanced. In the Hardings' example, this additional saving from better control of working capital would further increase profits to a revised total of £56,100, an increase of over 250 per cent on the originally stated profits of £15,000.

Assets

With regard to improving the perception of the quality of current assets, obsolete stock and bad paying customers should be weeded out at an early stage. Thus, when a potential buyer analyses these assets he will see the quality of the assets in a more positive light.

However, there are many other assets in a business. Some are more obvious than others. Most can be prepared in one way or another to improve the chances of a good sale. Consider first the principal or fixed assets of a business.

Property
Property is nearly always a significant factor when dealing with the purchase or sale of a business. Bearing in mind the improved profits from cancelling unnecessary maintenance work, property assets should not be allowed to deteriorate to such an extent that they need major repairs. Most sensible buyers will be more concerned about what can be achieved by using the assets than by what they look like. But they should look as smart as possible to provide the purchaser with a good first impression. However, a buyer will almost certainly seek a property survey and attempt to

obtain a reduced price if it has not been properly maintained. So common sense as regards maintenance needs to prevail.

If the business occupies leasehold premises then a buyer who intends to continue the business from the same premises will be concerned not only about its physical condition but also about the rent that has to be paid and the length of time for which there is certainty over that rent. If a seller is coming up to a rent review date, which may fall shortly after the date of the sale, it is worth considering bringing that review forward and agreeing the revised rental ahead of time. This increases the level of certainty that is being passed on to a potential buyer. However, it is not without some risk since it will probably commit the seller to a higher rent before it would otherwise have been necessary. In the case of a lease which is nearing the end of its term, it may be worth considering negotiating a new lease. For instance, if the lease has only two years to run it may be advantageous to negotiate a new longer-term lease even though the rent may be higher. This can have the added advantage of substantially reducing the landlord's potential claim for dilapidations.

However, all this presupposes that the property is an important factor to a potential purchaser. If a purchaser is likely to move the business from the existing premises to ones he already occupies then this type of consideration is unnecessary. But security of tenure and rent reviews will be a particularly important factor in the sale of retail businesses where location is generally a crucial consideration.

Surplus assets

A distinction should be made between those assets that are necessary for the continuation of the business and those that are surplus. It may well be that a buyer does not wish to purchase surplus assets and will not be prepared to pay best price for them. At an early stage in the process it is worth considering selling such assets separately or even restructuring the business so that those assets are held outside the business that is to be sold. An extension of this consideration is whether the operation that is being sold should be split into separate businesses. A hotel business that also owns a restaurant in an adjoining town may have more value if it is split into two separate businesses rather than being sold as one. A buyer of a hotel does not necessarily wish to take responsibility for a completely separate operation elsewhere. A buyer whose prime interest is the purchase of a restaurant almost certainly will not want to buy a hotel as well! By careful preparation it should be possible to structure the operations so that they can be sold either as one, if a buyer wishes it, or as two separate businesses. This will enhance the chances of a successful sale and may indeed increase the total price obtainable.

There are a number of other ways in which the assets of a business can be improved to enhance the price. Behind most of them is the principle of providing as much certainty as possible to a buyer as to the continuing profitability of the business. Certainty of future profits will increase the price that can be obtained.

The workforce

An important asset in most businesses is the workforce. Few businesses can operate without one. There may be key people who need to remain with that business if it is to be attractive to a buyer. After all, a buyer is not only purchasing physical assets but also access to a workforce that can produce income from those assets. Consideration should therefore be given to tying these key people into the business, possibly by providing them with more than the minimum terms (eg. longer notice periods on both sides) required for a legal contract of employment but probably more effectively by introducing a form of incentive scheme. If entered into early enough, this could be tied to the sale price achieved. However, this is particularly difficult when the owner does not wish to tell his workforce that the business is for sale until a deal is agreed. This is understandable since knowledge of a potential change of ownership can upset a workforce, creating unease and even distrust. This whole area needs to be treated with great caution. There is no standard guideline. Each situation will depend on the nature of the business, the present management style and the longer-term intentions of those owners who are involved in the management. But if you do have key people who are not involved in the 'sell' decision it is best to take them into your confidence as soon as you can.

Customers

Another asset that is an integral part of the business is the customer list. The more those customers can be tied into the company with long-term contracts the more certain the income of the company is. This is only feasible in certain types of business but should not be ignored.

Suppliers

If the business is dependent upon key suppliers a buyer of the business will be keen to know the terms on which these suppliers will continue to supply. Thus if contracts for supplies can be lengthened so that an element of certainty can be introduced for at least a period after a sale has taken place, this again establishes a level of certainty as regards costs. But beware! If a supplier is a possible buyer this is not recommended. A long-term supply contract given to a major supplier who also wants to buy the business could strengthen his negotiating position. Not being given the contract, however, may put him off buying altogether.

Any renegotiations to lengthen certainty must be realistic. Anything that ties the hands of a buyer in a way he does not wish is also likely to affect the price offered – downwards!

Licences

One other area needs to be mentioned. If either retailing or manufacturing within the business is to some extent dependent upon operating under licences from other companies then it is as well to make sure that the availability of those licences is extended as far forward as possible. Few people will wish to buy a business where a product is manufactured under a licence which does not extend more than a few months beyond a purchase date.

These then are some of the ways owners can prepare their businesses for sale with a view to obtaining a better price. There will certainly be some others, many of which will depend on the nature of the business being sold. It is worth giving a lot of thought to this area since good preparation will undoubtedly be reflected in a much better price.

5 *Taxation*

Whenever the sale of a business is envisaged there are important tax considerations which must be addressed. The seller should be concerned with the tax position consequent upon the sale because of the amount of tax to be paid. Furthermore, the timing of that tax payment directly affects the value to be derived from the disposal. The seller will wish to be assured that maximum advantage is taken of those reliefs from taxation which may be available.

However, it should always be remembered that the disposal of a business is primarily a commercial transaction. It can only be achieved between a willing seller and a willing purchaser at a mutually acceptable price. This price will normally be set in gross, or pre-tax, terms. In seeking to minimise his own tax liabilities, in whatever legitimate way that may appear to be appropriate, the seller should be careful to keep the transaction simple. There is a danger that introducing unnecessary tax complications at any stage, but particularly late in the negotiations, may jeopardise the successful conclusion of those negotiations. The purchaser may become suspicious of the seller's motives and concern about other aspects of the deal might then also rise to the surface. He may fear that the seller's proposals will work to his own disadvantage.

So taxation is important to the sale of a business, but equally it is sensible to keep matters simple or, at least, to ensure that they are clearly understood by both parties to the transaction. They can then be satisfied as to the consequences pertinent to themselves. Good professional tax advice, however complex the underlying concept, is only of value if clearly expressed, with both positive and negative consequences explained. If the advice given is not easily understood or the issues appear clouded, clarification should be insisted upon.

Of necessity this chapter, dealing with taxation, is bound to be a little more technical than others because of the nature of the

47

subject matter. However, the content will remain general, dealing with the broad principles. Tax advice in relation to any particular transaction must be tailored specifically to that transaction, and to the objectives of both the interested parties. Consequently, information given here can be no substitute for taking professional advice. This will generally be from an accountant or a lawyer whose explanations can be understood, and who can demonstrate that he has relevant and recent experience of the tax aspects of sales of other similar businesses.

It must be stressed that the reasons for sale (see Chapter 1) and what you are selling (see Chapter 2) are of paramount significance to the taxation issues which may arise. For the purposes of this chapter the total sale of a business is assumed. Various alternatives to a total sale were discussed briefly in Chapter 1 but the taxation consequences of those alternatives will not be dealt with here.

The disposal of the entire business of a sole trader or partnership gives rise to capital gains tax implications on the disposal of many of the assets (both tangible and intangible) and also to income tax implications consequent upon the cessation of the trade by the sellers. By contrast a limited liability company is a separate legal entity, and is therefore quite distinct from its owners or shareholders. Consequently the sale of a company does not constitute a business cessation for tax purposes. However, the sale of the shares in the company does give rise to capital gains tax implications for the selling shareholders.

Under current legislation, stamp duty is payable by a purchaser when buying a business. It might seem therefore that this is of no relevance to a seller. But in the eyes of the purchaser it is an extra cost which will affect the price he is prepared to pay. Thus a seller has a vested interest in a buyer finding ways to minimise the amount of stamp duty payable by the purchaser. Opportunities for minimising the stamp duty liability are more restricted in the case of a company than on the sale of the assets of an unincorporated business, but the rate applicable will be lower. In addition value added tax also needs to be considered carefully whenever a significant transaction is envisaged. However, if all the relevant conditions set down in law are satisfied the disposal of a business should not result in value added tax liabilities arising.

It is beyond the scope of this chapter to consider the gratuitous disposal of a business, such as the gift of a family business to succeeding generations. Consequently, inheritance tax implications which may arise in such circumstances are not considered. However, some brief comments on the seller's inheritance tax position following the sale of a business are pertinent and the chapter concludes on that point.

Whether the business being sold is that of a sole trader, partnership or limited company, capital gains tax is a key consideration. With careful planning to take advantage of the various reliefs or exemptions that may be applied, the amount of capital gains tax eventually payable may be significantly reduced. This will help to maximise after-tax sale proceeds for the seller.

Since capital gains tax is a complicated subject in its own right a broad outline of the main principles is given first, then more specific consideration of the various tax consequences for the seller on the disposal of a business carried on by him as a sole trader or in partnership. There then follows a similar resumé when shares in a limited liability company are sold.

Capital gains tax: the basic principles

Capital gains tax is chargeable on the disposal of assets whether they be tangible (such as land and buildings or shares in a company) or intangible (such as the goodwill). Where assets are sold the chargeable gain or allowable loss must be computed.

The detailed capital gains tax legislation has undergone significant changes in recent years and is now extremely complicated. No doubt by the time these words are read some further amendments to the legislation will have been enacted. As at the time of writing (December 1991) the computation of chargeable gains or allowable losses are broadly as set out below.

The computation commences with the sale proceeds, net of the direct costs of sale such as professional fees. Typically these may include the fees of lawyers, surveyors and accountants. From this figure the 'base cost' of the asset is deducted. Assuming that the asset was acquired after 31 March 1982, 'the base cost' is the original acquisition price paid together with any subsequent expenditure of a capital nature which has enhanced the value of the asset. This subsequent expenditure must still be reflected in the state or nature of the asset at the time of disposal. An example of this might be a permanent extension to a building.

The deduction of the 'base cost' from the net sale proceeds gives the net chargeable gain. From the net chargeable gain indexation relief is then deducted. This is an allowance for inflation, as measured by the movement in the Retail Price Index from the month of acquisition of the assets to the month of disposal. The appropriate indices for the period of ownership are applied to the acquisition cost and, where relevant, to the enhancement expenditure. Thus the 'base cost' is effectively index-linked. This means that capital gains tax is applied to real gains rather than inflationary gains. Indeed, indexation may turn a gain over original cost into a loss both in real terms and for capital gains tax purposes.

Sale of assets acquired before 31 March 1982

The position is more complicated where the asset being sold was acquired on or before 31 March 1982. Two computations of the chargeable gain are required: one by reference to original cost and the other by reference to the asset's market value as at 31 March 1982. Accordingly, it may be necessary to obtain professional valuations of assets held at 31 March 1982. In both computations the indexation allowance is based on the 31 March 1982 value (or cost if greater) and is determined by reference to the movement in the Retail Price Index from March 1982 until the month of the disposal. There is no relief for the effects of inflation prior to 31 March 1982. The result of the two separate computations must then be compared. Where both produce a gain, or both produce a loss, the lower gain or loss is taken. However, if one of the computations results in a gain, and the other a loss, then the disposal is treated as giving rise to neither a gain nor a loss for capital gains tax purposes.

Having computed the chargeable gain or allowable loss on the disposal of a particular asset, the position on all disposals made by an individual during a tax year must be added together to arrive at his net chargeable gains (or losses) for the tax year, which runs from 6 April to the following 5 April. Any capital losses which the taxpayer has brought forward from previous tax years and the annual exemption from chargeable gains (which is currently £5,500 for each individual taxpayer) may then be deducted. The balance is chargeable to tax, subject to any other specific reliefs or exemptions.

Under current legislation, the capital gains tax payable is computed on the taxpayer's net chargeable gains at the rate of income tax applicable to that individual for that tax year. At present, this will be either 25 or 40 per cent. Capital gains tax is due for payment on 1 December following the end of the tax year (ie. 5 April) in which the underlying disposals took place. This will be the tax year in which unconditional contracts are exchanged, which may be sooner than the tax year in which completion actually takes place. Thus when a disposal is contemplated close to the end of a tax year it may be sensible to defer exchanging unconditional contracts for a short while, until the start of the following tax year. As a result the payment date for any capital gains tax might be deferred for an additional 12 months.

Seller's emigration

Many of the reliefs or exemptions from capital gains tax which may be available are linked with the reason for the sale and are discussed below separately as they apply either to the disposal of an unincorporated business or to the disposal of a company. However, it is worth dealing here, as a general principle, with the position when the reason for sale is the seller's intention to emigrate. In such circumstances the disposal could fall outside the scope of UK capital gains tax altogether. The timing of events is all-important.

Emigration implies an intention by the seller to give up residence in the UK either permanently or temporarily and to take up residence abroad. An individual who is not resident and not ordinarily resident in the UK during a tax year is not generally liable to UK capital gains tax. But the seller should check the tax position in the overseas territory to which he is emigrating to ensure the disposal will not be taxed there instead. Broadly, to avoid being a UK resident in a tax year, one must not be present in the UK for 183 days or more in that tax year or make regular visits of three or more months per year over a four-year period. If one has a home available in the UK one should not visit the UK at any time in the tax year (unless working abroad on a full-time contract). The Inland Revenue may give a ruling that a person is not resident or ordinarily resident from the day following his departure.

Theoretically, it should be possible to emigrate and then to sell a business without liability to UK capital gains tax. However, the position is always scrutinised by the Inland Revenue very closely in such circumstances. They might contend that the sale was actually agreed before the date of emigration, even if not formalised until later. If so the capital gain remains chargeable to

UK taxation. If emigration is contemplated as a genuine reason for sale extreme care should be exercised and experienced professional advice sought to avoid taking any steps or failing to take steps which would reduce the benefit arising from emigration. In particular the rules covering disposal of a business or partnership interest are even tighter than those applying to the disposal of shares in a company.

The sale of a business by a sole trader or a partnership

When a business is sold by a sole trader or a partnership the sellers will be selling a range of assets. These may include land, buildings, equipment, fixtures and fittings, cars, stock and debtors. They may also be disposing of their business liabilities. They will almost certainly sell an intangible asset, namely the goodwill of the business. It is essential to understand what is actually being sold to appraise the taxation consequences, including capital gains tax, income tax, stamp duty and value added tax.

Once an overall sale price has been agreed there is normally scope for the seller to negotiate and agree with the purchaser how that figure should be allocated between the different assets that comprise the total business. This allocation will affect the tax position of both the seller and the purchaser and is therefore a point of considerable importance. It will affect the capital gains tax liability which may arise and the potential availability of reliefs from that tax. The value attributed to stock and work in progress and to equipment, fixtures and fittings will affect the final income tax liability of the ceasing business. It will also be critical to the buyer on the opening position for the new business.

The most appropriate allocation depends on the individual circumstances of each case. The overriding principle is that any allocation agreed must be fair and reasonable since it may be challenged by the Inland Revenue. It cannot be fixed purely to maximise tax benefits, but must reflect the underlying reality of the transaction. The same allocation must be adopted by both the seller and purchaser and ideally, to avoid subsequent debate, should be fully set out in the sale agreement drawn up by the lawyers.

The main taxes applicable on the sale of an unincorporated business are now considered in turn.

Capital gains tax

Typically, on the disposal of an unincorporated business, the assets to be sold which will give rise to capital gains tax may include land and buildings and goodwill. The capital gain or loss arising in respect of each chargeable asset must be computed separately and the results then aggregated.

The amount of the total sale proceeds allocated to the various chargeable assets will directly affect the net chargeable gains which may ultimately arise. In view of the range of reliefs from capital gains tax which may be available, depending on the particular circumstances, the seller may prefer a higher allocation of the consideration to chargeable assets. This could restrict the proceeds to be allocated to assets such as stock and work in progress affecting the final income tax liability, from which there may be less scope to apply beneficial reliefs.

The 'base cost' of certain of the chargeable assets being sold needs to be considered carefully. For instance, where the seller is selling a business that he started himself it is likely that originally there was no goodwill. Accordingly, there will be no 'base cost', and no figures on which to claim the indexation relief. However, if the business was started prior to 31 March 1982 a goodwill valuation as at that date may assist considerably. Where the sale of the business involves the disposal of premises held on a short leasehold basis (that is a lease of less than 50 years) the original cost that is allowable for capital gains tax purposes must be scaled down to reflect the diminishing value of the lease as it runs towards its expiration date.

Having arrived at the aggregate of chargeable gains or losses for the full range of chargeable assets involved in the disposal of the business, one should then look to the reliefs that may be available. Very often reliefs are related to the reason for the disposal.

Retirement relief

If the owner is selling because he wishes to retire, due to age or ill health, a significant relief from capital gains tax, known as retirement relief, might be obtainable.

Retirement relief is available once the relevant criteria set out below are met, whether or not the seller is actually going to retire (he could sell his business and obtain retirement relief from capital gains tax, but still carry on working in the business under its new management, perhaps to ensure a smooth handover):

- it is necessary to have reached the age of 55, or to be retiring earlier on the grounds of ill health. It must be one's own health that is the cause of the disposal of the business, and not that of one's spouse or any other person which may be affecting one's ability to carry on managing the business. The Inland Revenue will need to be satisfied that the business disposal is genuinely a result of ill health, and will require a medical certificate in support. They may also request a further medical examination. Once past the permitted age of 55, such medical requirements do not have to be met.
- the business must have been owned by the seller for at least one year and the maximum relief is only available if he has owned the business throughout a ten-year period. For periods of ownership between one and ten years the limits for the relief are scaled down on a pro-rata basis.

The maximum amount of retirement relief possible is the full amount of the first £150,000 of chargeable gains and then one-half of chargeable gains arising between £150,000 and £600,000. Accordingly, a maximum of £375,000 of chargeable gains can escape liability to capital gains tax. It is important to note that retirement relief is only available against the chargeable gains arising on the disposal of chargeable assets used for business purposes. If the business owns premises and rents out some surplus space, retirement relief will be restricted to that proportion of the premises which is used for purposes of the seller's business.

Retirement relief may also apply in respect of the disposal of assets owned personally but used in the seller's business. For instance if one partner owns premises used by a partnership for the purposes of its trade, he could be entitled to retirement relief in respect of his disposal of the premises. However, the extension of the relief to these circumstances is not available if the partner charges a rent to the business for the premises. If a rent is charged the premises take on the nature of an investment rather than a business asset.

Roll-over relief
Where the sale of the business is because the seller wishes to change direction and pursue new or different business activities, it may be possible to defer chargeable gains by way of roll-over relief. If the conditions for exemption under retirement relief and

for deferral by roll-over relief both apply, retirement relief is preferable. Indeed, it should take automatic precedence since, in theory at least, there is no need to claim retirement relief. It should be given automatically if the relevant conditions apply. In practice the Inland Revenue may need reminding!

Roll-over relief may apply on the disposal of certain categories of assets. The proceeds of disposal must be reinvested in replacement assets also falling within those same permitted categories. The reinvestment must normally occur within a period commencing one year before and ending three years after the date of the disposal of the original assets, but the Inland Revenue do have the discretion to extend this time limit in appropriate cases. The permitted categories include land and buildings occupied and used for the purposes of the trade (again this would exclude surplus premises rented out), goodwill, some items of fixed plant or machinery, ships, aircraft and hovercraft, milk quotas and potato quotas. Where the total proceeds of disposal are reinvested within the required period in suitable replacement assets, the chargeable gain may be rolled over. This means that the gain does not then become chargeable to capital gains tax at that time. Instead the amount of the capital gain is deducted from the base cost of the replacement assets for future capital gains tax purposes. This has the effect of deferring the current tax liability at least until such future time as the replacement assets are sold. However, at that time another roll-over claim might be made if further replacement assets are to be purchased, thus extending the deferral still further, and perhaps until such time as the seller becomes eligible to benefit from the retirement relief provisions.

Trading loss offset
There is a new relief from capital gains tax available to proprietors of unincorporated businesses, introduced with effect from 6 April 1991. Where the business has trading losses and the seller makes capital gains, including those made on the disposal of business assets, it may be possible to offset the trading losses against the chargeable gains, to reduce the amount upon which capital gains tax is charged. This relief is only available after taking into account the normal income tax provisions for relieving trading losses. These new provisions may be beneficial where a business is being sold because it is currently making losses, but there are some valuable business assets of interest to a potential purchaser.

Deferred payment of sales proceeds

In a number of instances the total sale proceeds may be paid to the seller over a period rather than immediately on completion. The capital gains tax liability still arises by reference to the date of exchange of contracts. However, where the proceeds are to be paid by instalments over a period exceeding 18 months the Inland Revenue may also allow the seller to pay the capital gains tax liability arising in instalments provided the Revenue are satisfied that the seller would otherwise suffer undue hardship. In many instances the amount of the deferred consideration may be contingent (for instance, on profit targets being achieved) and the final amount to be paid may be unascertainable at the time of the exchange of contracts. Here the position is particularly complicated. Tax is initially computed by reference to the sale proceeds immediately payable and also to the current market value of the right to receive the deferred consideration. The current market value of the right to receive the future consideration will be the subject of considerable negotiation with the Inland Revenue. When the deferred consideration is eventually received it will be treated as the chargeable disposal of the right to receive that further consideration. Professional advice is clearly essential.

The capital gains tax consequences of a business disposal are of vital importance. However, as can be seen it may be that the capital gains tax position of the seller can be mitigated significantly by the reliefs built into the legislation to assist business succession.

Income tax

Perhaps surprisingly, the income tax consequences of the disposal of an unincorporated business can be of equal or greater concern, depending on the facts and the exact taxation position of the seller. The disposal of an unincorporated business is generally treated as a cessation or permanent discontinuance of that business for income tax purposes, even if the same business is to be carried on in a similar fashion under new management.

As noted above the total sale proceeds must be allocated between the various assets of the business that are to be sold. The amount allocated to stock or work in progress will directly affect the profit (or loss) of the business in the final period of trading to the date of cessation or disposal. Some assets such as equipment, fixtures and fittings and also motor cars qualify for capital allowances, being allowances against income tax for certain qualifying capital expenditure. The disposal proceeds must be brought into the capital allowances computation. In the final period of trading, up to the date of the disposal of the business, excess proceeds might result in the Inland Revenue claiming back some allowances previously given to the taxpayer. Alternatively, when the proceeds are lower there may be a balance of allowances which will be given to the taxpayer.

Therefore the allocation of the sale proceeds not only affects the capital gains tax position but also the seller's income tax liability. The importance of allocating the sale proceeds wisely, but on a just and reasonable basis to minimise the risk of Inland Revenue attack, cannot be over-emphasised. Unfortunately, each case can only be considered in the light of individual circumstances and general rules as to the most appropriate allocation are liable to be misleading.

Generally sole traders and partnerships are assessed to income tax on a prior, or preceding, year basis. This means that the liability to income tax for the current tax year is based on the results achieved for the 12-month accounting period which ended in the preceding tax year (6 April to 5 April), and that profits which are generated this year will not form the basis of assessment to income tax until next year. This is generally advantageous particularly when profits are rising.

This favourable system comes to an end on the cessation or permanent discontinuation of a business. In the tax year of the disposal the actual profits from the start of the tax year (6 April) to the date of the disposal are assessed. That in itself is not a problem. The penultimate and pre-penultimate years will already have been assessed on the normal preceding year basis. However, the Inland Revenue have the option to change the basis of assessment for those two years from the preceding year to an actual basis of assessment. They calculate which basis results in the highest amounts being assessed to income tax. In practice where one has a thriving business with profit levels following a rising trend for each of the final three years the Inland Revenue will opt to alter the basis of assessment for the penultimate and pre-penultimate years from a preceding year basis to an actual basis of assessment. This is because the more recent, and higher, levels of profit, will form the basis of assessment for those years. Without careful planning, the seller will find that the disposal may have cost him an unwelcome and substantial income tax liability. Conversely if the reason for sale is that the business has been declining over recent years the Revenue will not opt for the penultimate and pre-penultimate years to be assessed on an actual basis. They will prefer to keep the older, higher profit levels on a preceding year basis, as those which form the relevant basis of assessment.

With the Inland Revenue controlling the decision over the basis of assessment, a business disposal may result in higher income tax liabilities for the final years and is unlikely to reduce them. However, the seller can exercise some control by careful choice of the appropriate date for the disposal of the business such that he controls which years of assessment may be open to adjustment by the Inland Revenue. This requires careful analysis of profit trends and profits achieved in different years.

Stamp duty

On the disposal of an unincorporated business there will be a liability to stamp duty payable by the purchaser at the rate of 1 per cent on the value of the consideration paid for the conveyance or transfer of assets, such as land and buildings, fixed plant and machinery, goodwill, debtors or investments held by the business. However, no stamp duty is payable in relation to assets which may be transferred merely 'by delivery' – that is without the need for a stampable document – such as most plant and machinery, stock and work in progress. Once again, the question of the apportionment of the sale proceeds between the various assets of the business is important. For stamp duty purposes the value of the consideration is not just the amount paid, but also includes the value of any liabilities of the business taken over by the purchaser. Accordingly, it is common on the disposal of a business to exclude the transfer of debtors and creditors. These remain the asset and liability of the seller, who may collect in outstanding debts and use the funds to pay off the creditors. In addition to the commercial benefits the effect is to reduce the value of the consideration which is liable to stamp duty.

There is an exemption from stamp duty where the consideration for certain dutiable assets does not exceed £30,000. Accordingly no stamp duty may be payable on the disposal of the smallest businesses. However, once the £30,000 *de minimis* limit is breached, stamp duty at 1 per cent is payable on the full value of the consideration for dutiable assets and not just on the balance in excess of £30,000.

Value added tax

At last some good news! Provided three vital conditions are satisfied, the transfer of all or part of a business as a going concern falls outside the scope of value added tax. Given the current level of the standard rate of VAT this is a valuable relief and, therefore, care should be taken to comply with the conditions. These are:

1. the assets are to be used by the purchaser in the same kind of business as that in which they were used by the seller;
2. the purchaser must be a taxable person or become one as a result of the transfer. A taxable person is one who is liable to be registered for VAT because his turnover exceeds the registration limits applicable at that time, whether or not he is actually registered, or who has been accepted for voluntary registration;
3. there must be no significant break in trading either before or immediately after the transfer.

HM Customs and Excise do occasionally challenge whether there has been a valid transfer of a trade as a going concern and whether the above three conditions for value added tax exemption have been satisfied. A successful challenge could be a disaster for the seller since he might then be required to account for VAT at the standard rate out of the proceeds received. This would greatly reduce the reward to him for the sale of his business. In seeking protection the seller should always insist that the sale agreement states that the consideration is 'exclusive of VAT, if applicable'. If VAT subsequently becomes payable the seller could then look to the purchaser to pay over VAT on top of the original consideration agreed.

Normally on the disposal of a business the seller will cancel his VAT registration, unless he has other businesses to which it is also applicable. If so wished the original VAT registration may be transferred to the purchaser to save him taking out a fresh VAT registration. However, the purchaser may prefer to start with a fresh VAT registration rather than inherit any obligations or liabilities of the former owner of the business.

The sale of a limited liability company by its shareholders

The sale of a limited liability company by its shareholders is a somewhat different proposition from the sale of a business by a sole trader or partnership. As we have seen the latter involves the sale of a whole package of different assets which collectively comprise 'the business', and for most tax purposes the allocation of the sale proceeds between those various component assets is a key factor. So far as the sale of a limited liability company is concerned, it is generally the case that only one asset is being sold. That comprises the shares in the company which may be owned by just one or by a whole group of persons. However, each seller is merely selling his shares. Accordingly there is no question of the allocation of the consideration between different assets. However, to the extent that there may be various different classes of shares in the company, entitling the shareholders to different rights, then shares in different classes may well have different values. The complexities which might then arise are beyond the scope of this book.

When considering the sale of a limited liability company it is again appropriate to comment on the various different taxes which might be involved. From the viewpoint of the seller, for whom this book is written, capital gains tax is the most important area to cover. There is no equivalent of the onerous income tax liabilities that might arise on the disposal of unincorporated business.

Capital gains tax
The disposal of shares in a limited liability company may give rise to a capital gains tax liability. It will be necessary to prepare a computation of the chargeable gain arising, as described earlier in the outline of the broad principles of capital gains tax. The 'base cost' will be the cost of the shares to the shareholders or their market value as at 31 March 1982, as appropriate. It is irrelevant whether the company may have bought or sold chargeable assets in the intervening time, since those are assets belonging to the company, upon which the company may or may not be liable to tax. They are not the direct property of the shareholders whose only asset is the shares in the company.

Having computed the chargeable gain arising on the disposal of the shares, the seller shareholder will be interested to know what reliefs or deferrals from capital gains tax may be available to him.

Just like the proprietor of an unincorporated business, a company shareholder may be able to use his annual exemption from capital gains tax to reduce the amount of the gain which may be chargeable to tax. A shareholder may have more scope to maximise the use of the annual exemption. It is easier to subdivide the disposal of a company into two or more transactions over more than one tax year. He might be able to sell some shares in one tax year and the balance of his shares in a subsequent tax year, using the annual exemptions of both years involved. At a time prior to the disposal he might have gifted some shares to his wife (a transaction exempt from capital gains tax). Both spouses could then use their separate annual exemptions. However, where the chargeable gain is calculated by reference to the 31 May 1982 market value rather than original cost, such a prior transaction could seriously reduce the 31 March 1982 market value and result in an increased chargeable gain liable to tax. This point further illustrates the need to take professional advice relevant to the particular facts and circumstances of each individual case and at an early point in the discussions about a potential sale.

It is possible that the seller shareholder will have capital losses from previous transactions which can be offset against the chargeable gain arising on the disposal of his shares. To this extent his position is the same as that of the proprietor of an unincorporated business.

Retirement relief

If the reason for the disposal of the company is the shareholder's wish to retire either on the grounds of age or ill health, retirement relief may be available. The basic rules as to the age limit (at least 55 years old) and ill health requirements, and the length of ownership criterion to determine the maximum potential relief (currently £375,000 after ten years' ownership) are the same as for the proprietor of an unincorporated business. As noted previously, the proprietor of an unincorporated business could only obtain retirement relief in respect of the disposal of business assets, rather than assets used for investment purposes. The same is broadly true for the shareholders of a limited liability company but to arrive at this position the situation is more complicated. Remember, they are only selling shares rather than a collection of assets. It is necessary to calculate the chargeable gains arising on the disposal of those shares and then look at the actual assets held by the company. The chargeable gain eligible for retirement relief is scaled down in proportion to the value of chargeable non-business assets or investment assets held by the company as a ratio of its total chargeable assets at the time of the disposal. To this extent the tax inspector looks through the 'corporate veil'.

In the case of an unincorporated business, retirement relief is available to a proprietor or to any of the partners who satisfy the basic qualifying criteria regardless of the proportion of the business that they actually own. Thus a 57-year-old partner who owns just 10 per cent of the business and has done so for more than one year will be entitled to some retirement relief. In the case of a company the rules are more stringent. The company must be a trading company and it must be that individual's family company. This means that either the seller must own at least 25 per cent of the voting rights in the company, or the seller's family must own at least 50 per cent of the voting rights and he must own at least 5 per cent. Some advance planning is frequently required to ensure that these more stringent ownership criteria are met for a sufficient period prior to retirement.

Where a shareholder satisfies the above criteria he may also gain retirement relief in respect of assets owned personally but used in the course of the business of his family trading company.

Roll-over relief

Roll-over relief in the form available to proprietors of unincorporated businesses who reinvest their sale proceeds from qualifying assets into suitable replacement assets in the stipulated time period, is not available on the disposal of companies. This is because shares are not included in the permitted categories of assets. Thus a shareholder who wishes to change direction by selling his company and purchasing another business is less favourably treated than the proprietor of an unincorporated business. (There is a very limited exception in the case of certain sales to employee trusts, but this is not of sufficient general interest to warrant further comment here.) He might be advised that his company should sell its trade and assets (while he retains ownership of the shares in the company) and that his company then purchases the trade and assets of another business. In this way the company might be eligible for roll-over relief whereas the shareholder would not be.

There is, however, a special form of roll-over relief that is available to company shareholders. This can apply where the consideration for the disposal of their shares is met by the receipt of shares in another company. Typically this might happen where a successful small business is taken over by a larger public company. Rather than pay cash the public company, which may well be quoted on the Stock Exchange, might offer the smaller company shareholders some of their quoted shares in exchange for the shares that they currently own in the smaller company. This is known as a *share for share exchange*, or a *share swap*. The result is that the small business becomes a subsidiary company of the larger quoted company and its former owners or shareholders would become shareholders (probably minority shareholders) in the larger public company. If the purchasing company is quoted, this can be attractive for the sellers since they could sell their new quoted shares on the stock market at some future time, when perhaps they need the cash. Indeed, they may be able to sell just a few shares each year, making use of each year's annual exemption from capital gains tax.

Where there is a share swap arrangement, so long as it is effected for proper commercial reasons and is not part of a scheme or arrangement designed for the avoidance of tax, the Inland Revenue will give advance clearance that no capital gains tax will arise at the time of the share swap. In broad terms the chargeable gain on the disposal of shares in this manner is deferred until the replacement shares are eventually sold.

One problem which often arises in practice is that retirement relief is not available on the disposal of the replacement shares in the quoted company. It is most unlikely to be the seller's family trading company as previously defined. Yet at the time of the share swap the seller shareholder may have been aged 55 or over and satisfied the other retirement relief conditions in relation to the disposal of shares in what was then his family trading company. Accordingly, had he sold his original shares for cash, capital gains tax on the chargeable gains arising might have been reduced by retirement relief. He could now be worse off, since when he sells his new shares he will be chargeable to tax, the amount of which will be increased by the deferral as a result of the share swap. To alleviate this problem, the seller can elect that the deferral provisions in relation to a share swap do not apply to him such that he is then chargeable to tax on the share swap but can take advantage of the retirement relief provisions.

Payment by instalments
Frequently the disposal of a company involves payment being received in a series of instalments. The taxation position can become very complicated and depends on the exact nature of the instalments. If from the outset the total final consideration is

fixed but is to be met by a series of payments over a period of more than 18 months, the Inland Revenue may allow the seller to pay his capital gains tax liability by instalments if he would otherwise suffer undue hardship. Where the amount of the deferred consideration is contingent on such factors as performance the actual amounts deferred are unascertainable at the time of the sale. Tax on the disposal is then computed by reference to the sale proceeds payable immediately, plus the current value of the right to receive the future payments. This figure will be the subject of negotiation with the Inland Revenue. When the further proceeds are eventually received, they give rise to a further capital gains tax computation, being based, theoretically at least, on the disposal of the right to receive that further consideration. This can give rise to a number of pitfalls and detailed experienced professional advice should always be sought before agreeing to any deferred consideration arrangements.

Deferred consideration deals may also involve consideration being paid by way of the issue of shares by a quoted company. In effect they are share swap or share exchange deals, but with an element of consideration contingent on the continuing performance of the company. In such cases the deferral of capital gains tax available on share swap arrangements until the disposal of the replacement shares may still be possible, but only as a result of a concession by the Inland Revenue. This concession will only apply to the extent that the sale agreement stipulates that the deferred consideration must be paid by the issue of further shares. There must be no cash alternative.

Income tax
Companies do not pay income tax. Instead they pay corporation tax on their taxable profits. However, where a director or shareholder receives income from his company in the form of salaries or dividends he is liable to income tax. It can sometimes be advantageous prior to the sale of a company for the shareholders to receive a substantial dividend to remove surplus cash and reserves from the company. This will reduce the value of the company that is to be sold and will therefore limit the capital gains tax that would otherwise be payable by those shareholders on the disposal of the business, in the absence of any suitable reliefs to mitigate the capital gains tax liability.

Although the rates of income tax and capital gains tax have, since 1988, been set at the same levels, the actual tax treatment of dividends confers a possible advantage on the recipient. When a shareholder receives a dividend of say £75, he is treated as also receiving a tax credit at the basic rate of income tax, which would currently represent £25 in this example. That gives him a gross dividend of £100 on which tax at the current top rate of 40 per cent (if applicable) would amount to £40. However, he can offset the tax credit of £25 giving him a net higher rate liability of £15, being just 20 per cent of a net dividend of £75. Had the seller been a basic rate taxpayer only, then he would not have any higher rate liability in respect of the dividend since the full amount of his income tax liability would have been met by the tax credits.

Theoretically, the value of the company will have fallen by the £75 net dividend on which the shareholder's maximum tax rate is just 20 per cent as illustrated above. Had that £75 of the value remained in the company it would, in principle, have increased the capital gain on which tax would have been due at 40 per cent (or 25 per cent as appropriate). However, the actual capital gains tax liability depends on the base cost of the shares and the reliefs and exemptions which might be available. Therefore it is always necessary to look at actual figures and circumstances before determining the optimum course of action to follow.

Although pre-sale dividends can be advantageous there are some points to watch. First, the company must have sufficient reserves available for paying dividends. Broadly, dividends may only be paid out of accumulated profits. Second, when a company pays a dividend it must pay over to the Inland Revenue an amount equivalent to the shareholder's tax credit. This is treated as an advance of the company's own corporation tax liability. It is essential to check that this amount can be set off against actual corporation tax liabilities arising on present or previous profits. If it cannot, the actual cost to a company paying dividends will rise by the addition of the tax credit for which the company has no immediate offset. In other words the advance corporation tax becomes an actual cost to the company rather than merely a cashflow consideration.

Sometimes on the disposal of a business the outgoing shareholder directors wish to retain assets which have been provided to them by the company as part of their remuneration and benefits package. Most typically an outgoing director shareholder may wish to take over the ownership of his company car. While in the sale agreement only a nominal value might be attached, for income tax purposes the director shareholder will be treated as having received a benefit equivalent to the current market value of the car at the time he takes it over.

Ex-gratia payments to outgoing employees or directors

Another problem area lies in the practice of making ex-gratia payments to outgoing employees or directors. There is a broad exemption from income tax in respect of such payments up to a value of £30,000. However, an ex-gratia payment made to a director at the same time as he is selling his shares in the company will normally be treated by the Inland Revenue as an additional payment to the shareholder for the sale of his shares and will be subject to capital gains tax. Particular care must always be taken with any unusual payments made to a shareholder on or close to the time that he disposes of his shares in the company.

Corporation tax

Corporation tax is not generally a matter of concern to the seller of an entire company. The concept of a permanent discontinuance of the trade which is applicable to the disposal of an unincorporated business, is simply not relevant. A company is a separate legal entity entirely distinct from its present owner. It carries on from a corporation tax viewpoint largely unaffected by any change of ownership. However, there can be some difficulties regarding the carry forward of trading losses where there is a change in ownership. Generally, these points are of more concern to the purchaser than to the seller, but the seller should note that where a company does have trading losses which may be used in future periods, these losses may be regarded as an asset of the company at the time of its disposal. He may be able to use the existence of unrelieved trading losses as a negotiating point to increase the value which he receives for the disposal of the company. However, where he has taken any action which might constitute a major change in the nature or conduct of the trade of the company within a three-year period prior to the change in ownership, the Inland Revenue may deny the use of trade losses as from the date of the change in ownership. Therefore major alterations to the business of a loss-making company should be avoided by the seller in the three-year period leading up to the sale of the company.

Stamp duty

On the sale of shares, stamp duty is payable by the purchaser at the rate of half a per cent. This is less than the 1 per cent rate applicable on the disposal of those assets of an unincorporated business to which stamp duty is applicable. However, although the rate is lower, it does apply to the full value of the consideration since all the consideration is payable in respect of the shares, regardless of the underlying assets.

Value added tax

Because the company is a separate legal entity, it retains its own VAT registration, despite a change in ownership. This is subject to any subsequent action which the purchaser might feel appropriate. However, a sale of shares should not give rise to a liability to account for VAT on the part of the seller. Where an individual is selling shares it is most unlikely that he will be a taxable person and thus the transaction will be outside the scope of VAT. If for any reason the seller is registered for VAT (perhaps because the company is being sold by another company – its parent company) the sale of shares would in most cases be an exempt transaction. Although it will not give rise to a VAT liability, it may have the effect of restricting the amount of VAT which may be recovered by the parent company making the disposal.

Tax indemnities and warranties

Because the sale of a limited liability company is the sale of a separate legal entity which retains its own separate existence despite a change in its ownership, the company also retains responsibility for any liabilities built up during the period of ownership of the sellers.

Accordingly, the purchasers of any company are likely to require the seller to provide suitable warranties and indemnities (see Chapter 8) against any liability to taxation which might subsequently come to light due to any act or omission by the seller during his period of ownership and management of the company. In a typical company sale and purchase agreement warranties and indemnities can run to many pages. It is always vital that the seller does not agree to, or sign, anything that he does not fully understand and that he takes full and clear advice in this area. Otherwise the disposal of a company may only signal the commencement of lengthy and costly litigation.

After the sale – what next?

The sale of a business can be a very emotional event. But the seller must adjust to the future and ensure that his tax and financial affairs are properly geared for that future.

There are any number of possibilities as to what the future holds in store – retirement, change in direction, emigration or whatever. The consistent factor is that the ownership of a business has now been exchanged for some other assets. Most likely it is cash, but possibly it is a minority holding of shares in another company. Plans must be made to adjust to these new circumstances and some thought should be given to inheritance tax.

Inheritance tax

Inheritance tax applies to the passing on of an estate on death and to certain chargeable lifetime gifts, particularly if made within seven years of death. Broadly, chargeable lifetime gifts and the value of one's estate on death must be aggregated to determine the value to which inheritance tax applies. Up to a total value of £140,000 there is a zero rate band. After that tax is payable at 40 per cent. There are a number of exemptions which apply both to lifetime transfers and on death, such as gifts to one's spouse or to charities. Also there is a lifetime annual exemption of £3,000 for each tax year. Clearly, the speed with which the seller acts to organise his affairs will minimise the inheritance tax liabilities which may eventually arise and protect his wealth for the benefit of future generations.

There is a special relief from inheritance tax under which the value of a business, or of assets owned privately but used in the business may be discounted by either 30 or 50 per cent depending on the exact circumstances. The detailed rules are not relevant here since the business has now been sold. What is pertinent is that following the business disposal the relief will no longer apply in most circumstances, and therefore the seller's potential liabilities to inheritance tax may be substantially increased. Even if inheritance tax planning has previously been undertaken, now is the moment to reappraise the position. If no previous planning has occurred, start now.

Surprisingly few people have made wills. Those who do have one do not always update them as regularly as they should in the light of changed personal circumstances. The disposal of the business may well be a catalyst for planning for the future by making, or revising, wills. This may be done as part of an overall inheritance tax review.

So the business has been sold, but there is still plenty of tax planning to be done to meet the seller's future needs and intentions.

6   *The Asking Price*

If the seller quotes an asking price he automatically puts a maximum price on the business when out there, somewhere, may be someone prepared to pay considerably more. So an important piece of advice is don't quote an asking price if it can be avoided. At some point in the negotiations a price indicator may have to be given but that is not the same as going into the market to sell the business with a price already attached. But as always with generalised statements, there are some exceptions. A need for a quick sale may require an asking price to be quoted early. Similarly, businesses that are based primarily upon leasehold retail premises will frequently be seen advertised at a price for the lease plus stock at valuation. This is not surprising, given that the sale of the lease is a property transaction, where it is conventional wisdom to quote an asking price. For many businesses though, it is best to avoid quoting an asking price up front.

Essentially, the value of a business is what somebody else will pay for it. Selling therefore is the ultimate test of a business's value. Given this, when thinking about selling as few assumptions about the potential buyers as possible should be made. It is particularly unwise to make assumptions about the motives of buyers, though in preparing for a sale it is necessary to assess who the most likely buyers will be. In the final analysis it is the buyer who places the value on the business not the seller. But that does not mean to say that a seller ought to go ahead with a sale without a clear idea as to what that value might be.

Target price

Before entering into the final selling process the seller should fix two prices in his mind. The first is a target price. This is the price which, if obtained from a purchaser, will leave the seller with a feeling of satisfaction, with a feeling that he has obtained the

70

financial objectives he set out for himself at the outset. This is not to say that it will satisfy his wildest financial dreams but, having taken into account the circumstances of the sale as discussed in earlier chapters, it will meet the sensible objectives that were set. If there was to be an asking price, then that should be higher than the target price.

Walk-away price

The walk-away price is the minimum acceptable to the seller. It is the price below which the seller will not enter into a transaction but will be prepared to hold on to the business for some time to come. Again, this walk-away price must be set at a realistic level. As for any pricing assessment it should take into account the real circumstances of the sale. For the same business one seller may have a higher walk-away price than another if, say, he has a longer time horizon. Setting this walk-away price calls for an honest and realistic appraisal of the performance of the business and the reasons for sale, particularly if they are related to ill health. It is of little use setting an unrealistically high walk-away price if a quick sale is required because of serious ill health. Naturally it is unwise for the seller to disclose what that price is to anyone except perhaps his closest adviser. If any of his advisers are to be involved in the price negotiations it is sensible for them to have an understanding of the minimum requirements so that they can take them into account during the negotiating stage. What the buyer will be trying to do is to work out what the seller's walk-away price is so that he can purchase the business for as little over that figure as possible.

Real value of price

Before going further it is as well for us to pause for a moment to determine what is meant by price. There are various ways in which a price can be paid, some of which can involve payments at future dates. An offer of £600,000, £200,00 of which is paid up front and £200,000 at the end of each of the first two years is not in reality an offer price of £600,000. By deferring payments the purchaser is denying the seller the use of that money for those periods of time. By making assumptions as to what income would otherwise be receivable by the seller or what capital gains might accrue if the money was invested, it is possible to get an indication of what that offer is worth in present terms. This is called the *net present value*. Taking a simple example let us assume that the seller had intended to invest the proceeds of the sale in excess of £200,000 in a bank account, the interest on which would have provided him with an income (before income tax) of £4,000 (that is 1 per cent) per month. In the first year following the sale the seller would be losing £4,000 per month income while in the second year £2,000 per month income. Taking account of this loss of income means that the offer is equivalent to an up-front cash offer of about £530,000. If £600,000 was his walk-away price, but on reflection he was prepared to accept deferred payments, then the two deferred payments in this example would need to be raised to approximately £240,000 to compensate.

It is by assessing offers in this way that it is possible to compare the financial terms of competing offers. But it is only an indicator since it does not take into account certain additional risks that may be involved in accepting one offer against another. For instance, in the above example there may be a risk that the deferred payments will not be paid when they become due. Indeed, if there are deferred payments the purchaser's ability to pay must be assessed.

Before setting any price, whether it be asking, target or walk-away, the seller needs to have an idea of the likely value of the business. Valuing a business is not an exact science and therefore any figures that are arrived at should be treated with caution. All valuations include assumptions about certain factors. However, despite the inherent weaknesses in valuations they are of great use if properly prepared. It is as well for a seller to take independent advice in considering the value since it is important to be both methodical and objective. Not surprisingly, owners can find it particularly difficult to be the latter.

The principal ways of valuing businesses prior to sale are by reference to the profits of the business, to its assets or to alternative entry costs to that business. Let us consider each in turn.

Valuation by reference to profitability

A buyer who is prepared to pay for a business on the basis of its profitability will seek to assess, prior to purchase, the level of profit that can be generated in future years by that business as presently constituted. The assessment will be based on the present business and will not include, in normal circumstances, improvements which the buyer himself can make to the business. The purchaser will be buying a maintainable level of future profits to which he will then add his own expertise to generate additional profits. It is now that the benefits of spending time preparing for sale by improving the profits will surface. Two principal factors will be taken into account when assessing *future maintainable profits*:

- the actual profits being generated at the present time;
- the trend of profits over recent years.

Very different values will be placed on businesses which have the same current level of profits but where the trend in profits has been significantly different. If there is no reason to believe that the profit trend will change in the short term, a higher value will be placed on a business with a profits growth of 25 per cent per annum as compared to one with no profits growth at all.

Maintainable profits and profit trends

In attempting to value a business on a profits basis the first step is to calculate the normal level of profits of that business. In Chapter 4 reference is made to various steps that could be taken to improve levels of profitability and to isolate details of various items of discretionary expenditure. When arriving at a valuation based on profits, adjustments can be made for items of discretionary expenditure which have not been eliminated. The extent to which they can be added back to the actual profits of the business must depend on how easy it would be to save that expenditure in the future and the ability to provide relevant supporting evidence to a potential purchaser that each item is truly discretionary and can be saved.

Discretionary expenditure is not the only item that needs to be taken into account when assessing normal levels of profit. In assessing both current profit and profit trends, adjustments need to be made for items or events which may have been unusual within the business. If in a particular year a biscuit manufacturer made a profit by carrying out one large transaction, buying and selling flour, such profit would be taken out of any assessment of maintainable profits. Similarly, if in the year of sale the business had ceased a part of its activities, the profits or losses relevant to those activities in past years would need to be eliminated, since they are not going to be a factor in the future profitability of the business. On an even more detailed level, if certain product lines had been eliminated from the business then the effect of those lines, particularly on the current year's profits, should be adjusted. In all likelihood the products will have been eliminated because they were loss makers and such adjustments should therefore be beneficial. But if there are future costs still to arise in respect of any such cessation of business, these should be deducted from any valuation arising from an assessment of future maintainable profits.

To take a simple example consider Jackover Limited. This company has manufactured biscuits for many years. In 1990 it carried out a one-off trade in flour which it obtained unusually cheaply from an overseas supplier. Then, during 1991, Jackover ceased to import a line of slimming biscuits which had failed to make an impact on the market during the three years that they had been imported. The profits shown by the business over the three years 1989 to 1991 were £90,000, £145,000 and £120,000. However, when the figures are looked at more closely they show that the profits were in fact generated as follows:

	1989 £	1990 £	1991 £
Profit/(Loss)			
Biscuit manufacturing	95,000	113,000	138,000
Slimming biscuits	(5,000)	(3,000)	(18,000)
Flour sale	–	35,000	–
Total profit	£90,000	£145,000	£120,000

The only part of the business that is continuing is the biscuit manufacturing side. Its profits have in fact increased over the three year period from £95,000 to £138,000, which is a considerably more impressive performance than just looking at the total profit figures for that period.

Another factor that should be taken into account is *inflation*. The profit increase from £95,000 to £138,000 two years later is a high growth rate, in excess of 20 per cent per annum. If in fact that growth rate had been nearer 7 or 8 per cent, then this would indicate no real growth in profits over the period since inflation was at that level. In real terms that would have meant that there had been a flat, rather than a growth, performance. This would affect the value placed on the business.

Interest charge

In the above example profits were shown after charging all expenses and interest. In assessing the profitability it is important to look closely at the interest that a business has to pay for any borrowings that it has. Consider two companies, A and B. Both make profits, after interest charges, of £100,000. In the case of Company A there are no interest charges, as all the funding for the business is provided directly by the shareholders. However, in the case of Company B half the capital required for the business is provided by way of bank overdraft. If the total funds invested in each of the businesses is £700,000 the situation can be illustrated as follows:

	Company A	Company B
	£	£
Shareholders' funds	700,000	350,000
Overdraft at 14.25% interest	–	350,000
	£700,000	£700,000
Profits before interest and tax	100,000	150,000
Interest	–	50,000
Profits before tax	£100,000	£100,000

What this shows is that on pure financial grounds Company B appears to be a better business. It generates 50 per cent more income in respect of the funds employed in the business than Company A, that is £150,000 as against £100,000. Given that purchasers of businesses decide for themselves how they will fund that business, the maintainable profits before interest and tax are generally of greater interest in a valuation than the figure for profits after interest. We will return to these two companies again in a moment.

The multiplier

Having determined the level of maintainable profits, the next stage in a valuation is to decide what multiplier to use. Or to put it another way, how many times maintainable earnings will a purchaser pay?

Price/earnings ratio

One of the most common comparisons in looking at the relevant values of businesses is the price/earnings ratio (PE ratio). On the business pages of certain newspapers, price/earnings ratios are shown for many of the companies quoted on the International Stock Exchange in London. In general terms these indicate the price of the relevant share as a multiple of the after-tax profits per share earned by that company in its previous financial year. If a company has an indicated price/earnings ratio of 10 and a quoted price per share of 150p, the company has earned an after-tax profit of 15p per share (150 divided by 10).

It may be possible to find companies which have shares quoted on the Stock Exchange that are in a similar business to the one being sold. If so one can then use that PE ratio as a guide to a usable multiplier. Rarely, however, is it so simple. There are a number of difficulties, some of which can be overcome but others of which cannot. Though in a few cases it may be possible to find a truly comparable quoted company, in general this will not be so. The seller may have to rely on information in respect of similar companies but which are also involved in other businesses. The *Financial Times* publishes a series of indices based on the share price and profitability of companies that are in similar businesses. Various averages, including one for a PE ratio, are quoted. This will normally be a better indicator than using one for a particular company.

Price/earnings ratios are calculated on published accounts after taking tax charges into account. They are not based on maintainable earnings. Since the tax situation of companies can vary materially, this significantly affects the ability to obtain true comparisons. For example, in 1991 two similar companies in the same line of business each earned profits before taxation of £1,000,000. After tax, however, their profits were £710,000 and £960,000 respectively because the second company was able to set off losses it made in 1990 against its 1991 profits, while the first had no such losses to set off. If both were valued at £7,000,000 the PE ratios would be 9.85 and 7.29 respectively. This illustrates the danger of using a multiplier based on the PE ratio of any one quoted company unless it is comparable in all respects.

A further useful feature in having access to the PE ratio of a quoted company is that if the purchaser itself is a quoted company, it is unlikely to be prepared to pay a price which produces a PE ratio in respect of the business being bought which is higher than that quoted for the purchaser itself. This would be an indicator of the maximum price that might be obtainable from that potential purchaser.

Profits before interest and tax

So if the price/earnings ratio is a somewhat inaccurate multiplier what is an alternative? That most frequently used is a multiplier of profits before interest and tax (PBIT). While available statistics on values based upon PBIT are less easily accessible they can still be found. Companies can be selected in a similar line of business which have either been sold recently (and where one knows the price paid) or which are quoted on the Stock Exchange. By looking at their most recent accounts it is possible to arrive at a PBIT and compare that to the price paid for the company or the value of the company as quoted on the Stock Exchange. This gives a guide to the multiplier to be used in valuing the business to be sold.

Whatever multiplier is arrived at after such research it will be a reflection of the market's view of the industry. If it is an industry with a large growing market and therefore significant potential for expansion the multiplier will be higher than for a business in a market with low growth prospects. A higher multiplier is also likely to be indicated where the business is in a stable sector rather than a volatile one. For example, stable profits from a food processing company are likely to be more highly valued than volatile profits from a house building business.

To summarise, if a business is to be valued on the basis of profits it is necessary to establish the recent profit trends, the level of future maintainable profits, both before and after deduction of interest, and a multiplier that fairly reflects market sentiment as to the nature of the business. In the case of Companies A and B such research might determine that a valuation would lie somewhere between five times PBIT and seven times profits before tax. Company A would therefore be valued at between £500,000 and £700,000 while Company B would be valued at between £700,000 and £750,000.

Valuation by reference to assets

Valuing a business on the basis of the assets in that business is easier to accomplish. When it comes to a sale, a valuation on this basis is most likely to be relevant if the business is heavily asset based, such as a property investment company or a hotel business, or if it is a business that has a very poor profit performance. Consider once again Company B from the previous illustration. Set out below are the assets and liabilities of the business which in this case is structured as a limited company.

	£	£
Freehold property at cost		50,000
Plant, machinery and equipment:		
at cost	275,000	
less depreciation	125,000	
		150,000
Motor vehicles at cost	52,000	
less depreciation	17,000	
		35,000
		235,000
Current assets	550,000	
less current liabilities	285,000	
	265,000	
less bank overdraft	350,000	
		(85,000)
		£150,000

Company B's accounts show that it has a surplus of assets over liabilities of £150,000. However, that is not the whole story. Let us consider each category of asset separately.

Freehold property

Note that the freehold property is shown at the original cost to the business. However it was bought many years ago and has been adequately maintained. Given that property values have undoubtedly risen since, the figure of £50,000 shown is not a realistic assessment of its true value. So the directors of Company B call in property valuers to advise. But then the question arises as to the type of valuation that is required. A valuation can be expressed in a variety of ways, all having rather different meanings. Some of the most common phrases are 'with vacant possession', 'between willing buyer and willing seller', 'forced sale basis', 'for insurance purposes' or 'for mortgage purposes'. While a forced sale basis would be relevant if the business was about to go bust, that is not the case here. The most suitable valuation in this example would be on a 'willing buyer, willing seller' basis. So the directors of Company B obtain such a valuation. This values the property at £250,000, a surplus of £200,000 over the cost. This then is the value which should be borne in mind when assessing the asset value of Company B. It also means that the net asset value of the business is £350,000 rather than £150,000, subject to the valuation of other assets.

Plant, machinery and equipment

The two most usual methods of valuing plant, machinery and equipment are on a 'forced sale' and on a 'going concern' basis. The basis for the former is fairly clear. The value will reflect the estimate of the price obtainable if the business is broken up. The going concern basis is more subjective. It attempts to reflect the value of the equipment to somebody who is going to continue the business as it is. The valuation will be influenced considerably by the alternative cost of setting up a plant from scratch. If the equipment is highly specialised then the differences between the two can be considerable. On a forced sale there may only be a limited number, if any buyers, whereas on a going concern basis the fact that the plant is specialist and possibly difficult to replace makes it more valuable.

One real life example will illustrate the difficulties of valuing plant and equipment.

Company XYZ was in serious financial difficulty. It was a specialist contractor which could produce holes in metal to extremely fine tolerances without using drills. It worked primarily for the aerospace and defence industries. It used highly specialised equipment but despite the specialist nature of its business it was still unable to produce adequate sales. The directors sought a valuation of the plant and machinery on both a forced sale and a going concern basis. The valuers, one of the best known in the business, assessed the forced sale value to be £490,000 and the going concern value to be £920,000. (These values are expressed in terms current at the time of writing since the situation arose some years prior to this.) In the event the company ceased to trade and the equipment was put up for auction. It actually realised over £900,000 at auction indicating the valuers had seriously underestimated its forced sale value. The true going concern value will never be known.

In the majority of cases, if the depreciation charge properly reflects the reduction in value of the equipment as it grows older then the net value expressed in the accounts is likely to be close to its going concern value. This is the case with Company B. In the case of motor vehicles it is much easier to compare a value stated in the books of a business with the market value. There is a big second-hand vehicle market which enables one to assess the cost of replacing with similarly used vehicles or the price available from dealers. In this example, £35,000 is a fair reflection of value.

On the assumption that the stated value of £550,000 is a true reflection of the value of current assets, then the true net asset value of the business is £350,000. This is considerably lower than the value arrived at when valuing Company B on the basis of its profits. However, if Company B's profits before tax had only been £10,000, the asset-based valuation would be of much greater relevance.

As mentioned earlier, if it is a sole trader or a partnership selling a business, the liabilities legally remain those of the individuals concerned, whereas, if it is a company being sold, the liabilities remain liabilities of the company. In the example above the business was a limited company, and so net assets (that is the assets less the liabilities) were referred to. In reality the business of sole traders and partnerships may also be valued in this way since a purchaser may undertake to meet the business liabilities of the seller. However, even if that undertaking is given, it does not of itself mean the liabilities move to the purchaser rather than remain with the seller. Achieving that requires the agreement of each individual creditor of the business. Frequently this is not considered worthwhile, due to the delay involved and the possibility of upsetting certain suppliers with such a request. Furthermore, certain types of supplier – for example gas, water and electricity companies – are most unlikely to agree.

Deferred and contingent liabilities

Apart from the more obvious categories of creditor there are two others that need to be taken into account in a valuation. They certainly will be by a potential buyer, whether the business is a company or not. These are deferred and contingent liabilities.

A deferred liability is an existing liability of the business but the timing of payment of which is not known. The most usual deferred liability is taxation, since the payment of certain taxes can be deferred for considerable periods of time. This is not the same as paying a liability by instalments on fixed dates since on those occasions the timing of payment is known.

A contingent liability is one that may or may not become an actual liability. One example is where a company has guaranteed a liability of another company. That guarantee will only become a liability of the first company if in fact the second company does not actually pay. Another example is where there is a legal action claiming damages against a business. That will only become an actual liability if either the business accepts that it is liable or the case is decided against it in court.

If either deferred or contingent liabilities exist then a buyer will undoubtedly take this into account when considering the price he is prepared to pay. Thus a seller would be wise to take them into account when considering his own target and walk-away prices.

Certain types of asset-based businesses can be valued by reference to their earning capacity. For example, pubs are frequently valued on the basis of their turnover and medium-sized hotels by reference to both their turnover and to the number of their bedrooms. It is because there are many ways of looking at asset valuation that professional advice should be sought.

Valuation by reference to entry cost

There are some businesses which on the face of it are sold for what appear to be unrealistic prices – they may even be loss making and possibly have rather specialised assets. Two examples illustrate this point; the first is a paper manufacturing company, the second a business developing a new technology.

Paper manufacturing tends to be a highly cyclical business but one which requires enormous investment. A new paper mill might cost £100m; therefore the opportunity to buy one that is already in production with modern equipment at a lower price can be attractive. A purchase may be made regardless of whether the mill itself is making money for the present owners. The reason for the purchase is that the assets are being bought for a price lower than it would cost to build a new plant.

There have been many examples, particularly in the computer and electronics industries over the last 15 years, where a company has set out to develop and market products based on a new technology. After a time, the potential of that technology and developments therefrom made by the company may have considerable value to other businesses even though the original company may have made no profits or, more probably, fairly heavy losses. The attraction to a buyer is the advantage he will gain through taking on board the developed technology rather than having to start over again himself. He therefore may be prepared to pay a significant sum to achieve this advantage.

In both these cases the value of the business depends upon a comparison with the cost of starting up from scratch. That is what is referred to as an entry cost.

While a value can be placed upon a business in this way the real test is whether there will be anybody in the market-place wishing to buy it. By their very nature these businesses tend to be ones with a high asset cost or a long development period. In both cases there tend to be few potential buyers, which makes such businesses difficult to market. There is a great risk that there will indeed be no buyers and that therefore the business is effectively valueless. This is particularly true of high technology development situations.

Goodwill

So far in this chapter the question of the value of goodwill has been avoided. However, owners of many businesses believe, rightly, that the goodwill of their business has real value. In order to determine how that goodwill is valued it is important to understand what goodwill is.

In essence it is the value of the business in excess of the value of that business's assets (including such intangibles as patents and copyrights). Thus if a business is worth no more than the value of its assets then there is no goodwill value. To illustrate, consider again Companies A and B. The figures below summarise the net asset position of both companies at the time of sale.

	Company A	Company B
	£	£
Freehold property	250,000	250,000
Plant, machinery and equipment	150,000	150,000
Motor vehicles	35,000	35,000
	435,000	435,000
Net current assets	265,000	265,000
	700,000	700,000
Bank overdraft	–	350,000
Net assets	£700,000	£350,000
Estimated value	£500,000–£700,000	£700,000–£750,000

It can be seen that while Company A has no goodwill value, that for Company B is somewhere between £350,000 and £400,000. This reflects the fact that while both show net profits before tax of £100,000, Company A uses twice as much of the shareholders' money (or net assets) as does Company B.

The seller should note that though an asset, goodwill is intangible. It is harder for a buyer to raise money against it than, for example, on the security of a freehold property. This may limit the number of potential buyers.

While it is possible to embark on a detailed discussion on valuing goodwill, it would become highly technical. What is really important is to remember that the value of goodwill will generally reflect such factors as the level of profitability, the strength of the market position and whether the business is people- or asset-based.

Franchises

The principles behind valuing a franchise business are really no different than for any other business. What does have to be borne in mind is that if the valuation is to be based on profits it is heavily dependent upon the franchisor being prepared to grant a new franchise agreement to the purchaser. This can limit the marketability of the business and may therefore be reflected in a lower multiple of profits when valuing it. However, this is frequently compensated by the fact that the stability of the profits can be comparatively high. This results from the strong marketing support given by the franchisor and the management information it has available. If, however, the business has to be valued on an asset basis because profitability is low it may be difficult to obtain much more than break-up or forced sale value. And this may reflect the true reason for sale – pressure from the franchisor because of poor performance.

These then are some of the most important considerations that arise when trying to assess the value of a business. The work done to help provide a proper indication of that value can only be as good as the information available. More importantly, it can only serve as an indication of value since when the time comes to sell, various factors outside the control of the seller could affect the price. The most important benefit to the seller that arises from considering the value of a business prior to its sale is the help it gives in fixing a target and a walk-away price, through reference to solid information and sound advice. This should avoid the seller's sights being set too high or indeed too low. But as already stated a seller should avoid fixing an asking price if at all possible.

7   The Sales Memorandum

When it comes to marketing any product or idea there is generally
a need for marketing literature. Selling a business is no exception
to this. Before setting out to stir up the market in order to find
buyers, some time needs to be spent on preparing a sales
memorandum. The purpose of this memorandum is to provide
sufficient information about the business to enable prospective
purchasers to determine whether or not they wish to go ahead
with more detailed enquiries and discussions. It should not be
mixed up with a much bulkier document that may be issued in
respect of larger sales, frequently referred to as a business profile.
How the issuing of a sales memorandum fits into the overall
marketing process is covered in Chapter 8. The purpose of this
chapter is to deal with the type of information that should be
included in the memorandum.

The length and format of a memorandum will depend to some
extent on the nature of the business being sold. It may consist of
little more than a single sheet of paper with details not dissimilar
from those contained in an estate agent's handout. This could be
particularly relevant to the sale of a small business based on a
single retail property. In contrast, the sales memorandum may be
a summary of the larger business profile. But the purpose of both
these documents is the same – to help market the business to
would-be buyers.

The preparation of a sales memorandum is not as easy as it
sounds. It should be as brief as possible and yet contain the right
type of information for potential buyers so as to exclude those
who clearly will not be real buyers. This helps to avoid spending
a lot of time chasing up blind alleys. The memorandum should
contain at least some information that is not available from
public records but care needs to be taken to ensure that this does
not include commercially sensitive information. It is important to
bring out the plus points of the business but equally important not

to be overly bullish. Naturally, owners must avoid including statements which they know are wrong or which they cannot support with hard evidence. However, it is perfectly reasonable to refer to any potential benefits a purchaser might obtain, such as use of excess storage space or production capacity.

As already mentioned, the detailed contents of a sales memorandum will vary depending on the nature of the business that is being sold but many of the features outlined below will be relevant to most situations.

The business

The first thing that a reader will want from a sales memorandum is a general understanding of the nature of the business. It is extremely frustrating to a potential buyer not to be told early in the memorandum what the business actually does. Expecting would-be purchasers to look at audited accounts attached as an appendix for such information will not give a favourable impression. There should be a brief description of the product or service range, manufacturing or service capabilities, the type of customer who buys the products or services (though actually naming any of the customers should be avoided) and the locations at which the business operates. It may also be relevant to briefly describe the company's history, particularly its recent history, if it helps to illustrate a fast growth rate and/or a strong market position.

Ownership

There should be a clear statement of ownership in the memorandum. If the business is a partnership or a company the memorandum should state whether the whole business is for sale or not. If it is intended that one or more of the partners or shareholders continue with the business, this should also be stated. This will save time and energy by eliminating those only prepared to buy 100 per cent of a business.

Reasons for sale

At some point in the negotiations a potential buyer will undoubtedly ask why the owners are selling. Therefore, it is wise to include in the sales memorandum those reasons that the owners are prepared to disclose. In some cases it is more difficult to be totally frank about these and every situation has to be dealt with on its merits. Given that the memorandum is a marketing document, every attempt should be made to avoid implying that the seller is under pressure to sell, even if that is in fact the case. To make such a disclosure would be to hand a potential buyer a significant negotiating advantage. However, care must be taken not to mislead a potential purchaser as to the nature or value of the business, whether by including a statement or by omission.

Management and employees

Brief details of management and a summary of the employees within the business should be included. This will help a potential buyer to determine whether there is a continuing management team or whether the buyer will be expected to inject new management. It will also give an initial indication as to the nature of the workforce, for instance, whether it is a highly skilled one or not. Where a company is being sold and there are non-executive directors, their roles in the business should be mentioned.

Assets

In some cases it may be relevant to describe the company's fixed assets, particularly if these have a strategic importance. It may be that the production plant is 'state of the art' or even unique. If one is selling something like a hotel business then brief details of the property should be included.

Financial summary

When providing financial information for the memorandum the purpose of the document should be kept firmly in mind. There is a tendency to include too much financial information, increasing the opportunity for a potential purchaser to look at it out of context. Thus this section should include a summary of the trading results for at least two, but no more than three, of the years prior to sale plus management figures for the current year up to the latest date possible. Where applicable the figures should be adjusted for items such as excess directors' remuneration and other proprietorial expenditure. It is here that the work done to isolate the figures for discretionary expenditure referred to in Chapter 4 is important. Such a summary is illustrated below.

Summary of Trading Results (£000)

	Year to 31.12.89		Year to 31.12.90		10 months to 31.10.91	
	£		£		£	
Sales		640		820		760
Manufacturing costs		350		430		400
Gross profit		290		390		360
Marketing and administration		120		130		120
		170		260		240
Interest	50		80		55	
Directors' remuneration	60		125		50	
Exceptional expenditure	35		25		5	
		145		230		110
Net profit before tax		25		30		130

A summary such as this should then be followed, if necessary, by a brief commentary highlighting any particular points of relevance. For instance, in this example, it might be stated that the directors' remuneration in each year included a bonus paid once the results for the year were known and that the exceptional expenditure referred to marketing and travel costs incurred by the directors. Setting out the information in this way enables a potential purchaser to note that the business generated profits of £120,000 and £180,000 in each of the two completed years and £185,000 in the ten-month period, subject only to the cost of employing someone, if necessary, to replace the directors.

After the summary of trading results there should follow summarised balance sheets or statements of assets and liabilities as at the end of each of the two previous years. These should be adjusted for any assets that are not included in the accounts but will be sold as part of the business, such as a property owned directly by a shareholder of a company. Adjustment should also be made for assets that will not in fact form part of the sale, such as excess property which the owners wish to continue to own as an investment. And there is that Rolls–Royce which the owner wishes to retain! Similarly, adjustment should be made for any tangential business which is to be sold separately.

Finally, within the financial summary there should be some mention of future prospects. The owners should be extremely reluctant to give any financial projections in the memorandum other than, possibly, some in connection with the current trading year. And only then if that current year is nearing completion. The inherent danger of making projections for the future is that a purchaser will seek to obtain from the seller a statement within the contract that such profits will in fact occur. Attached to this will be a penalty if they do not. This will be referred to again in the next chapter when dealing with warranties. Mention can be made about the present order book and reference made to prospects, but avoid quantifying these if possible. Once negotiations commence, a purchaser will nearly always wish to get a management view of prospects. But the owner should generally ensure that the purchaser makes up his own mind about future prospects and does not rely on the owner's statements.

Either within the financial summary or as a separate section in the memorandum, reference can be made to potential future developments. These will, of course, be those developments planned by the present owners and may in fact be of little relevance to a potential purchaser. If, however, expenditure has been incurred in respect of these developments then some reference to it should be made.

Preparation

Generally, the sales memorandum will be prepared by the owners with substantial assistance from their lead advisers. Unless the management of the business has first-hand experience of the selling process, they would be well advised to let professionals help them. Good advisers have plenty of experience in drafting sales memoranda in such a way as to attract potential buyers with the minimum amount of information. If advisers do assist in the preparation of the document, then, assuming their reputation in the market-place is sound, the document will gain access where others might not. Many purchase opportunities are introduced to potential buyers by their own advisers – be they accountants, solicitors or merchant banks. These advisers will know those who are experienced advisers in the selling of businesses, who know the process and who prepare digestible sales memoranda. One from a recognised source will get a fair reading, while others may not.

Disclaimer

Whoever issues the memorandum should ensure that it contains a disclaimer or that it is sent with an accompanying letter which details the basis of its preparation. This will state, among other things, that the document has been prepared by the directors or owners of the business, that it has been prepared from current information available, but that it does not purport to be a prospectus. Such disclaimer should make it clear that the owners do not guarantee or warrant the information contained therein and that prospective buyers must make further enquiry. Remember, the memorandum is a marketing document and does not and should not hold itself out to present the business, warts and all.

If an adviser sends out the memorandum he should include an extremely strong disclaimer stating that all the information has been provided by the owners of the business, that he, the adviser, takes no responsibility for it and that he has not verified any of the information. This is standard practice to protect both the owners, the directors and the advisers and should not be a cause of concern. Any professional advising a potential purchaser will not be surprised to see such disclaimers included. Indeed he would be surprised if they were not.

The Financial Services Act 1986 regulates the issue and approval of advertisements as defined (which a sales memorandum in respect of a limited company is likely to be) to entice investors into a business. In certain instances – for example, where the business is not a limited company or where one purchaser buys the controlling interest in a private company – the regulations may not apply. Because of the complexity of the requirements and the sanctions if breaches occur, owners and directors should take professional advice before issuing any letter, document or similar which could be construed to be an advertisement. The rules are tough and should not be ignored.

The business profile

As mentioned earlier, when selling some businesses a business profile (also referred to as an information memorandum) is prepared. It is of particular importance in situations where it is intended that potential buyers will have to indicate the terms and amount of their offer for the business prior actually to entering into detailed negotiations. As might be expected, this generally relates to larger businesses. The profile will expand considerably on the information that would be included in a sales memorandum. In particular, it would give much more information on customers, competitors, suppliers, future developments and the management and organisation. It would also have more detailed historical financial information, probably going back at least five years. They may also include details of significant contracts, both with customers and suppliers.

Given the detailed information involved the cost of preparation, not only in respect of external advice and help but also of management time within the business, can be high. In the case of smaller businesses, therefore, the preparation of such a document should be avoided.

8 *Finding A Buyer*

Having gone through the thought processes and preparation work set out in previous chapters, the point will arrive at which the seller wishes to set about finding potential buyers. Other than in exceptional circumstances the aim will be to find a number of potential buyers, one of whom will eventually purchase the business. To achieve this the seller's activities should now be directed towards creating a market for his or her business. The reasons for interesting a number of different parties are fairly obvious.

When negotiating a deal it is easier to negotiate from a position of strength in the knowledge that there are a number of people who wish to buy the business. If there is only one potential buyer and the owner is keen to sell then his negotiating position is clearly weak. With a number of potential buyers around there is a greater chance that the seller will achieve most of his pre-set objectives. Put another way, he is more likely to receive a satisfactory price, however that is expressed, than if there is only one potential buyer. Furthermore, the seller can turn to one of the other interested buyers should the favoured purchaser fail to go ahead with the transaction for one reason or another.

In deciding how to find the buyer the seller should have a clear view as to what the characteristics of a potential buyer are likely to be. If a seller's sole interest is the amount of money that will be paid over on completion of the transaction – ie. he is not concerned about the future of the business, nor does he want to receive deferred payments – then clearly his prime concern will be that any potential buyer has sufficient cash to pay for the business. A seller may be particularly concerned about the future of the employees and is prepared to take a lower cash price in order to achieve as much security for them as possible. This may preclude selling to purchasers whose interest is to expand market share and exploit economies of scale, since this generally means that there will be significant job losses. Indeed, with smaller companies it frequently means that manufacturing processes and such like are moved into the buyer's own factories, with the attendant loss of jobs.

The ability to find a suitable number of potential buyers to maximise the price can be severely constrained if the seller wishes to maintain a high level of secrecy. It is obviously impossible to sell a business unless people are actually told that it is for sale. If the seller wants to interest a number of different parties then that must widen the number of people who are going to know. Secrecy is then increasingly difficult. However, there may well be considerable justification in being concerned over secrecy, particularly in relation to customers, competitors and the workforce.

Customers may become disconcerted if they know that the owner in whom they have put their faith to date is actually trying to get out of the business. The workforce may become increasingly unsettled not knowing the effect that a potential sale will have on their future employment. It is certain that direct competitors, if they are aware of the situation, will use the information to increase their own market shares by sowing seeds of concern within the customer base. So concern over secrecy is natural and in a few cases secrecy really is critical. This does however have to be balanced against the need to generate interest among potential buyers. The level of secrecy required can impact on which methods of finding potential buyers are used, as will be shown shortly.

Potential buyers

Before actually making contact with potential buyers, some time should be spent determining who those potential buyers may be. Allowing for any constraint that the nature of the transaction or of the objectives to be achieved by the seller may impose, the usual categories from which potential buyers arise are competitors, suppliers, customers, new market entrants, external management teams, the incumbent management team or complete 'wild cards', ie. the world at large.

Competitors

A competitor may wish to buy a business to expand his own business either by having a greater market share in the same locality or perhaps to widen geographical coverage. He may be looking for synergy between the two businesses and the ability to make savings as a result of economies of scale. By having an additional business he may be able to buy more cheaply from his suppliers because he can buy in greater bulk. He may be able to make savings by eliminating duplication between his existing business and the one that he is buying, particularly among head office and other administrative functions. It can also occur in respect of sales forces where savings can be achieved by cutting out duplication of manpower. A more cynical reason can be that the competitor just wishes to eliminate competition from the market-place and is prepared to take out a competitor even if it costs money. Inevitably, this will mean effective closure for the business being sold. However, it is unlikely that this route will be taken if the business being sold is a good one with a strong reputation in the market place and among its customers. By closing the business the risk of losing customers, particularly shortly after purchase, would be far too costly.

Having analysed who among the competition may wish to buy, the seller may decide that there are some to whom he would not wish to sell. For instance, the seller may be aware that a particular competitor could not pay for the business and therefore his sole reason for entering negotiations would be industrial espionage. More emotional reasons for an owner to refuse to sell to a competitor are because they have been arch rivals or just because he does not like the people. More usually, however, there is a real concern about the future of loyal and long-serving employees should certain competitors buy. All this must be taken into account when deciding which competitors, if any, are to be approached.

Suppliers

Suppliers are not the most obvious purchasers of a business. If a supplier buys one of its own customers then its other customers may be rightly concerned that the in-house business is getting supplies on better terms. If that were the case customers would perceive this as an unfair advantage in the market. Therefore, any supplier buying a customer has to weigh up the advantages against the risk of losing other customers. A supplier of raw materials who decides to get into a manufacturing business using that raw material, may not be subject to the same risk. Raw materials tend to be a commodity-driven operation, with high volumes and low margins. Prices are also extremely susceptible to economic cycles.

Manufacturing involves added value with potentially greater stability in both sales and profits and therefore there may be a natural desire to diversify into manufacturing.

If the business is a significant customer of a particular supplier, the supplier may be concerned that the business will fall into the hands of a competitor who uses a different supplier, which would therefore significantly harm his own business. The reason for a purchase by a supplier, therefore, is often defensive in nature but a perfectly valid one for a seller of a business to exploit if the opportunity arises. Overall, however, suppliers to the business are far less likely to be a purchaser than are competitors.

Customers

Among the business's customers there may be one or more who would be interested in buying the business. Again this will depend, as with suppliers, on the nature of the business and the importance of the relationship between the business and the customer. The more dependent the customer is on the business as a source of supplies the more interested he is likely to be in purchasing the business. Not surprisingly though, it is a major step for a customer to take and it is likely to be fairly evident at the outset of the sale process whether or not there is a real opportunity of a sale to a specific customer.

New market entrants

One of the most difficult categories for potential buyers to get at, or indeed to identify, are those concerns who may wish to buy the business as a strategy for developing new markets. These buyers may be companies whose own products are complementary to those of the business for sale. Or it may be that they are used for similar purposes. Or the customers of both companies may be similar and therefore the same type of sales force can be used for both activities.

However, new market entrants does not just apply to buyers getting involved with different products for the first time. There may be companies who produce the same or similar products but are not seen as competitors to the business for sale because they are not in the same geographical market. This is a particularly lively topic at present with the rapid development of the Single European Market and there are many potential buyers outside the UK for certain types of business. This interest is not confined only to the large businesses; a fair number of overseas companies come into the UK wishing to buy a small company in the first instance, as a foot in the door. The buyer may then have a strategy to develop a much larger business once they have got to grips with the UK business environment. Realistically, a business with a value of less than, say, £1 million is unlikely to be of interest to an overseas company unless it occupies a particular niche in the market-place or has specialist expertise not readily available elsewhere.

A third group of buyers in this category is the conglomerates. These are companies or groups of companies which have a number of diverse businesses. Sometimes there is a real strategy behind the variety of businesses owned but sometimes it has arisen only as a result of opportunism. One of the arguments for developing conglomerates is that they build up a portfolio of different businesses. Thus if one type of business enters a difficult trading period, this will possibly be balanced by better results elsewhere in the portfolio. Theoretically this should bring greater stability to the overall group. Again it is a particularly difficult group to get at as potential buyers unless they have made public details of the types of business for which they are looking.

Management teams
In the UK the 1980s became the decade of the management team buyers, and *management buy-outs* (MBO) and *management buy-ins* (MBI) became phrases in common usage. A management buy-out involves selling a business to the management team that already runs the company, whereas the buy-in involves selling a business to a completely separate management team, who generally have the support of financiers. Identifying the existing management team is easy, but the real question is whether that team is a professional management team that can operate without the involvement of the owner. If it is not an all-round team then it is unlikely that they will be able to interest financiers sufficiently to raise the sum necessary to take over the business. In this case it might be possible to buy-out in conjunction with additional team members brought in from outside. The transaction then becomes a mixture of a management buy-in and a management buy-out (sometimes referred to as a BIMBO). Identifying management buy-in teams who would be interested in buying the business is much more difficult. Unless the owners have had a direct approach from external management teams,

they will certainly require the assistance of professional advisers to identify potential purchasers in this category.

There are real advantages to an owner in selling a business to the incumbent management team. Negotiations can be quicker and will generally involve fewer loose ends. The owners should be able to avoid giving some of the more extensive undertakings normally required both as to the past activities of the company and its future profitability. Only exceptionally will an incumbent management team have sufficient cash to be able to buy the business outright and therefore they will need to interest backers. This can take time and will certainly limit the price that they can pay for the company. Complications may arise when an incumbent management team are interested in buying the business, as these same people will not be interested in talking to other potential buyers. Human nature being what it is they may even unintentionally disillusion the buyers, thereby reducing the price that the buyers are willing to pay. It may therefore be wise for a seller, if he is interested in selling to the management team, to give them an opportunity to buy at an early stage, with a specific time limit by which they must have achieved completion of the transaction. The downside risk of this tactic is that the owner will almost certainly have to quote his asking price and in reality the owner is not creating a market for the business. However, there are many businesses, in particular people businesses, where this route is a sensible one to pursue.

To reduce the risks the seller associated with an MBO attempt would be wise to have detailed discussions with advisers as to whether an MBO is a realistic route. If it is not, it is better for the seller to make it clear at the outset that there will not be a sale of the company to the other members of the management team. It is then up to the owners to maintain a positive relationship with the team so that the business is not undermined by people defecting prior to a sale. Whether or not certain individuals are tied into the business by means of special contracts must depend upon their importance to the ongoing business. This in turn depends on assessing what the intentions of a would-be buyer will most likely be.

A potential sale to a non-incumbent management team (an MBI) should be treated by the seller just like a sale to any other third party. It is particularly important at an early stage, however, for the seller to be certain that the management team has real financial backing. Otherwise the seller could find himself drawn into detailed negotiations with a party who may not be able to pay, having given up the opportunity to sell to some other party.

Wild cards

The 'wild card' refers to potential buyers of the business that could not have been realistically anticipated when putting the business up for sale. By their very nature they are the hardest to identify and are likely to arise either as a result of having advertised the business for sale or through word of mouth. It is worth spending a few moments to try and determine what type of buyer might fall into this category for the particular business that is being sold. But it is not worth spending too long.

Identifying potential buyers

Having established the categories from which potential buyers are most likely to come the next stage is to attempt to identify who those potential buyers may be.

First, there will be those individuals known directly by the seller. This is particularly the case when considering competitors, suppliers and customers. Each contact should be considered carefully, particularly the level of that contact within the potential buying business. Indeed, throughout the selling process it is important to try to make sure one is in contact with the people who actually make the decisions.

Second, there will be the contacts of the advisers. Most will have at least some contacts with potential buyers. Those advisers who are most heavily involved in the mergers and acquisitions business should have fairly wide contacts both within the UK and overseas. These may arise directly from their merger and acquisition activities but they may also arise from other activities within their overall business. For example, while an accountancy firm may have contact with a number of potential purchasers as a direct result of being involved in merger and acquisition activities, they do have an ongoing client base, some of whom could be potential buyers. They are also likely to have contact with other accountancy firms who have their own client base, which can be contacted if desired. If the latter route to reaching additional contacts is taken it is important to make sure that duplication of approach is avoided.

Third, potential buyers can be identified through research. Having earlier considered the categories from which potential buyers are likely to come, researching various sources of information available can identify specific businesses within that category. The seller is likely to have access to directories which provide some information on competitors as well as on potential suppliers or customers not already known to the seller. Information about them can be analysed in exactly the same way as that about known suppliers and customers. Computerised databases, to which many of the principal advisers on mergers and acquisitions have access, are especially useful among the many other sources of information available.

While research will not identify who is actually in the market looking for a business it can identify businesses which may be interested and are therefore worthy of approach. How much research is undertaken will depend on the level of existing knowledge either with the seller or with the advisers when creating a list of contacts. If the initial list arrived at through direct knowledge is already large then additional research may not have to be undertaken, at least in the early stages. If, however, the number of potential buyers arrived at through direct knowledge is limited then a much higher level of research should be undertaken.

Advertising is the fourth way of identifying potential buyers. The extent of advertising will depend on the objectives set for sale and the perceived requirement for secrecy. The most generally used form of advertising is taking space in a national or trade newspaper. This can be done by way of a small classified advertisement using a box number or by taking a larger amount of space and perhaps advertising through an adviser. The latter has the advantage that potential purchasers will feel safe in the knowledge that the sellers are being advised by known merger and acquisition advisers. Rightly or wrongly buyers tend to see this as reducing the risk of their time being wasted if they respond to the advertisement.

Whichever type of advertisement is placed and whatever the medium used, it is usual to state in the advertisement that only responses from principals will be considered. This helps to avoid having to deal with intermediaries who are only responding speculatively without representing a particular purchaser. This can cause a considerable waste of time to sellers and their advisers.

Apart from advertisements in newspapers and periodicals there are other ways of disseminating the fact that a business is for sale. Most specialist merger and acquisition advisers have their own mailing lists as well as access to joint computerised databases.

Information can be disseminated widely without actually publishing it in the press. Again, the particular details of these networks vary from adviser to adviser but are a well-tried route for identifying potential buyers. Whether formal or informal, these networks are particularly useful for identifying overseas buyers since any alternative method of advertising would be exorbitantly expensive except for the very largest of transactions.

But do not forget the requirements of the Financial Service Act 1986 as regards the issuing of *investment advertisements*. This is a very broadly defined term which not only includes newspaper advertisements but also mailshots, press releases, and other forms of advertisement. Take professional advice.

Contacting potential buyers

The method used to make specific contact with the potential buyers identified will depend to some extent upon how they have been identified. Except where interested parties are identified through advertising, the seller and their advisers should agree how each potential buyer is to be approached. Some might be sufficiently well known to either the seller or his advisers for contact to be made directly by telephone But there are strict regulations under the Financial Services Act concerning making contact by telephone about a business for sale, even between close friends. In most circumstances an unsolicited or 'cold' call of that nature is not allowed. Thus the most usual first approach will be in writing. It is important that the letter is sent to an identified individual. If it is not known who will be the ultimate decision maker it is wise to send it to the managing director, chief executive or chairman – by name. To have proper impact it is important that the person is correctly named and therefore the latest information available should be checked. A quick telephone call to the potential purchaser will act as a double check on names before the letter is sent. The more personalised a letter is the greater its chance of being read by the recipient.

In some cases it may be possible to use a third party, who is well known either to the seller or to his adviser, to make contact with a potential buyer. This may be because the personal level of contact between the third party and the potential buyer is particularly strong or in order that a certain level of secrecy can be maintained in the early stages.

Whatever method of contact is decided on it should be agreed before doing it and then carried out according to plan. The wording to be included in a letter should also be agreed beforehand to make sure the same message and information is sent out on each occasion. Since at this point nobody has entered into any form of agreement on confidentiality, care must be taken as to what information is divulged.

Where potential buyers have been found as a result of advertising then clearly the initial contact has already been made. Efforts should be made to try, as far as possible, to work out whether the respondents to the advertising are real prospective buyers. Response rates vary, but generally among those received will be agents and go-betweens who are looking for opportunities to find buyers who will pay them commission or who will seek to charge commission from the seller if they bring a buyer to the table. This type of response is best avoided, which can be partially achieved by including in the advertisement such wording as 'only principals to reply'. Then there are cranks and timewasters. Most are easy to spot, such as the embezzler who replied to an advertisement on prison paper! Sifting through replies is another area where an experienced adviser will save the owner a lot of time.

If the response rate has been high it will be necessary to prepare a shortlist of those who are to be dealt with first, while the others are kept on hold.

Confidentiality

Once the initial contact with potential buyers has been made a list of contacts who are showing a positive interest in buying the business and who, on the face of it, are acceptable purchasers to the seller, should be created. Those so listed will require further information. Before it is provided an agreement should be obtained from each of them regarding confidentiality of the information that they will be receiving and the use to which they can put it. This is generally done by way of a *confidentiality agreement* or *confidentiality letter*. There is some doubt whether or not the terms of these are legally enforceable either in theory or in practice. It will depend on the circumstances at the time whether the seller will wish, or indeed feel able, to mount an action for damages should confidentiality be breached. However, the signing of an agreement or letter between the parties undoubtedly creates a strong moral obligation. Experience shows that such agreements are generally honoured. Standard wording can normally be used thus avoiding the need to renegotiate the terms of confidentiality with every potential buyer. There may be some instances when special terms need to be used, particularly in the case of supplying information to competitors.

The principal contents of a confidentiality agreement are:

1. An undertaking by the potential buyer to treat information received as private and confidential. There will also be an undertaking that every effort will be made to keep such information private and confidential in the future.
2. A statement that the information can only be used for the purpose of evaluating whether the potential buyer wishes to proceed with negotiations.
3. A limitation as to whom else the information can be disclosed. This will normally be limited to the officers of the company or the partners in the business, employees who have to have the information in order to enable an evaluation to be made and specified advisers to the potential buyers.
4. An undertaking by the potential buyer to ensure that those to whom the information is supplied by them in the furtherance of the evaluation will comply with the limitations set out in the agreement.
5. An undertaking to keep a record of those to whom the information is disclosed.
6. An undertaking to return all the information and any copies made thereof to the sellers on request.

It would be quite normal and justifiable for a potential buyer to insist that confidentiality only relates to information that is not publicly available. Confidentiality would then not relate to information that has been filed in respect of a company at Companies House or information that has been released or commented on in the press. From the seller's point of view it should be made clear to the potential buyer that the agreement does not give any undertaking or warranty as to the quality or accuracy of the information that is being provided within its terms.

With certain parties, particularly competitors, there is a need to be very specific about what information will be released under the confidentiality agreement. Certainly until such time as a potential buyer is perceived as a front runner it is important to avoid the release of specific know-how and technical information. Information, such as terms of trade with customers, may be equally as sensitive, especially when dealing with competitors, and even tighter control of what information is passed over needs to be exercised.

Release of information

The first stage in the release of information will be to release the sales memorandum which has been prepared beforehand (see Chapter 7). Along with the sales memorandum there will normally be a request that a response be made by a given date. How strongly one makes that request will depend upon the level and quality of reaction one is getting from the market-place. It is not sensible to have a tough deadline if the sales memorandum is only being sent to one potential buyer because no others can be found. Whatever deadline is set, it is important that either the seller or the advisers follow up the potential buyer with direct contact after a few days. This way the seller may obtain some feedback as to the real level of interest. Telephoning is the preferred method here since verbal rather than written communication will be a significantly better gauge of the strength of interest.

The shortlist

On the assumption that a positive reaction is received from several potential buyers, some criteria need to be used to decide with whom negotiations are to be entered into on a more detailed level. Entering into a large number of different negotiations will be time consuming. If the seller is in the enviable position of having many potential buyers wishing to continue negotiations it is reasonable to seek from them an indication of the price that they would consider offering on the basis of the information that they already have, as well as the conditions that they would attach in making such an offer. This will enable the seller to reduce the number of potential buyers with whom negotiations will continue to an acceptable number. There are some risks to this approach: potential buyers may indicate a highly inflated price in order to make sure of being included in that later list, while others who might be more solid purchasers but who have given a more realistic price could be excluded. Great care therefore needs to be taken in assessing how genuine the quoted prices are.

If a considerable number of interested buyers are expected from the outset, then the process by which indicative offers are obtained at a comparatively early stage can be formalised. This involves those who have satisfied the seller and his advisers with the credibility of their interest meeting a predetermined timetable. Once confidentiality letters have been signed they will be given access not only to the sales memorandum but also to the much fuller business profile. They may also be given access to, though not copies of, a variety of legal documents and financial information to check out. Then by a specified date they will be required to make offers for the business. These offers will almost always contain conditions but they are made on the basis that the seller can accept them and that therefore the potential purchaser will be legally bound to proceed if their conditions are met. It will be for the seller and his advisers to decide whether a high offer which contains many conditions is preferable to a lower offer which has far fewer conditions. This formalised auction process is normally more suitable for larger transactions, particularly if there is significant interest from companies based in other countries.

Having interested a number of potential buyers and obtained positive feedback as a result of the information issued to them, the skill of a seller and his advisers is to keep the number of potential buyers with whom full-scale negotiations are entered into down to as few as possible without running the risk of having no back-up should the principal negotiations fail.

9   The Negotiating Process

Negotiating the sale of a business with a prospective buyer may be quick and easy. However, that is rarely the case. The process starts as soon as a sales memorandum is sent to prospective buyers – the document that is designed to raise a potential buyer's interest. From that point negotiations will continue right up until binding contracts are exchanged between the parties. In the early stages a seller may be negotiating with a large number of parties, in which case there is need of help from advisers who have the expertise to filter the early stages. If not, management's time will be taken up in negotiations while the business itself may suffer from lack of attention.

The aim of whoever negotiates the sale, be it the principal or the adviser, is to filter the hopefully large number of responses down to a few serious buyers and ultimately to one single buyer. To achieve this there are a number of negotiating stages. Every case will be different but if negotiations are taking place with more than one party there will be considerable similarity as to the way they develop. Of course, any potential buyer can drop out of the negotiations at any time. Whether or not the seller attempts to bring them back to the table will depend on how many others are continuing to negotiate at that time.

Negotiation stages

The first stage is to persuade a potential buyer to state a price together with his conditions. This may involve a number of meetings and the provision of additional information not contained within the sales memorandum. The extent to which additional information is provided will depend on how well negotiations are proceeding. Once the seller has a feel for the initial price that will be offered and some of the conditions that will be attached it is easier to determine how serious a potential buyer really is. Furthermore, this is the clearest way of assessing whether the work that has previously been carried out to determine the value of the business is in fact being reflected in the negotiations. By knowing at least the opening offers of the potential buyers a seller will be able to separate out those who are not even close to the walk-away price! This assumes, of course that there are some who are quoting a price higher than the walk-away price! So stage one is to get a good indication of a potential buyer's first offer and the conditions that are likely to be attached.

Second-stage negotiations require a seller to be rather more forthcoming about the price he hopes to achieve. The seller will possibly have had indications from a number of potential buyers of their first offer price and will be able to reassess both his target price and, if necessary, his walk-away price before giving such an indication. What is important is that, whatever the seller now quotes as the price for the business, a clear message is given to the potential buyer as to why the seller believes his price is the correct one. Simply quoting a price without some substantiation may be offputting to a number of potential buyers, and they may even consider that the seller is just flying a kite and is not a serious seller of the business.

This second stage is also a good time to clarify the conditions that the potential buyers are likely to attach to their offers. It will give time for the seller to decide whether he is going to find these acceptable and to assess to what extent they may delay the selling process. If a quick sale is looked for, this is particularly important.

The third stage is one of reassessment. After a time there should be a number of potential offers on the table. It is time for the seller to reassess them in terms of price and conditions. He needs to assess the likelihood of a particular potential buyer increasing an offer and changing conditions which are not acceptable. Where there are sufficient potential buyers it is time for the seller and his advisers to assess the ones most likely to succeed on acceptable terms. It is worth setting this analysis out on paper in some detail to identify the areas of difference, whether it be price or conditions. Alongside this, an assessment can be made of how keen the buyer seems to be to actually do a deal. Think about why the buyer may want the business and what his alternatives may be if he did not buy. By such analysis a seller can make some assessment of the most likely buyer and his top price.

The fourth stage is to reduce the number of potential buyers to the one with whom contractual terms are going to be negotiated.

At what stage this is achieved will depend on circumstances. Sometimes it is wise to reach this stage early, but to keep other potential buyers interested if possible. On other occasions the choice may be delayed right up to the final pre-contract signing stage. Certainly it is unwise to decide too early since if the preferred buyer is lost then the next in line will anticipate getting the business for a lower price. Whichever course of action is taken the seller will almost certainly reach a point where Heads of Agreement are signed with one potential buyer (see page 111).

Methods of payment

Among the principal items to be negotiated for inclusion in the Heads of Agreement will not only be the price to be paid and the conditions attached but the method by which payment is to be made. The tax consequences of various methods of payment are referred to in Chapter 6. However, good commercial reasons for choosing one method of payment rather than another must outweigh tax considerations.

Cash

The most uncontroversial method of payment is cash. Payment on completion by cash or, more normally, banker's draft, is the most sure way the seller has of getting his money. (A banker's draft is effectively a cheque drawn by a bank on its own account.) He not only gets his money but he knows when he is getting it. Indeed, for some of the reasons for sale referred to earlier this will undoubtedly be the priority method of payment.

Shares

Cash is not the only means of payment. If the purchaser is another company an alternative method of payment is by way of shares in that company. Whether or not payment by shares is acceptable is likely to depend on why the business is being sold in the first place and the quality of the buyer. There is a big difference between receiving shares in another private company and receiving shares in a well-known company with a listing on the International Stock Exchange.

Consider the situation where payment is by shares in another private company. Unless the seller is intent on being an active player in the new combined company then taking shares might be a considerable risk. The shares will not be marketable, and therefore transferable into cash, except with the agreement of the other shareholders. It will also be difficult to know what price may be obtainable for the shares at any particular time or whether anyone will buy them. If one reason for the original sale was to try and avoid the 'all eggs in the same basket' syndrome then certainly taking shares in the purchaser as payment does not achieve that objective. However, it might be achieved if payment was by a mixture of cash and shares. In general, however, the seller ought not to accept shares in a private company unless he will have an active role to play, can influence the decision making and it meets his original selling objectives.

The situation is somewhat different if the shares of the purchaser are quoted on the Stock Exchange. Such shares will have considerably greater marketability than those in a private company. However, if the number of shares that the seller is receiving means that he will own a significant part of the quoted company then selling the shares may not be as easy as he thinks. It is surprising how limited is the marketability of shares in a great number of quoted companies, other than the very large ones. This needs to be checked out carefully before agreeing to this method of payment. In addition, if as a result of the transaction the seller does become a significant shareholder in the quoted company then some of the conditions attached may place a restriction on how soon the shares issued to the seller may be sold. This in itself can be a severe constraint on the seller in realising the full cash value of his business. In all cases of payment by shares rather than cash, the overriding feature is that the seller risks those shares reducing in value while he continues to own them.

The taking of shares as payment can in one instance be similar to receiving cash. This is where, primarily in the case of a quoted company, shares are issued to the seller but against undertakings that they will be immediately sold, or placed, with a number of other parties, often financial institutions. Thus, effectively the seller is receiving shares in the purchasing company but is immediately selling them on and obtaining cash. This method will be used by a purchaser keen to issue more shares on to the market. But again tax considerations for the seller are important to assess, particularly if retirement relief from capital gains tax is a consideration.

As mentioned in Chapter 5, any transaction involving payment partly or totally by way of an issue of shares in the purchaser has considerable tax implications, some of them to the seller's advantage and some of them to his potential disadvantage. Good advice throughout the negotiations is important.

Deferred payments

There are many instances where the purchaser will require that the seller accepts part of the payment on a deferred basis. Whether or not such a condition is acceptable to a seller depends on his selling objectives. Assuming that it is, the most important factors for the seller to negotiate are to keep the deferred period as short as possible and to ensure, as well as he can, that payment, whether in cash or shares, will be made on the due date. Deferred payments will always be a feature of the transaction if in reality part of the payment is dependent upon the ongoing profitability of the business being sold.

The extent to which a seller will seek to enhance the certainty of payment will depend on the financial strength of the purchaser. It is as well for a seller to have done some research to ascertain the financial welfare of the purchaser. If the owner is selling out to a large publicly listed company then the chances are that that company will still be in existence when the deferred payment is due and will be able to meet the payments. However, as periods of recession have shown, this is not always the case, even with a company of that anticipated strength. If in doubt the seller should seek to have the deferred payment guaranteed to improve the certainty of payment. Undoubtedly the best method is to obtain a bank guarantee for the payments. But this may not be available. The seller could seek to take security over certain assets of the purchasing company to cover the potential value of the deferred payments. If the purchasing company has sizeable borrowings from its bank it may be difficult to obtain such security but it is certainly worth trying. Another method is to require the purchaser to obtain insurance cover for the payments. This is a specialised market but such cover may be available in the right circumstances.

Whatever method is used to enhance the certainty of the deferred payment actually being made it is worth trying hard to get it. If the purchaser does fail before payment is made then, unless the seller has additional security, the sums due will rank alongside all the other general claims in the liquidation or bankruptcy of the purchaser.

Earn-outs

Earn-outs refer to a method of payment whereby a significant part, if not all, of the price is deferred and is dependent upon the future performance of the business which is being sold. This has become a popular method of payment, particularly at times when prices paid for businesses are high in the expectation that their future profits are going to grow at a high rate. It is for that type of business for which the earn-out is most suitable. There are many variations to the earn-out formula. Sometimes there will be a significant up-front payment with top-ups over each of maybe two or three years thereafter. Sometimes the future payment will be a single sum at the end of the designated period, perhaps with an upper limit on it.

Apart from high growth businesses it is also a particularly useful method of payment for the purchaser where he needs to retain the services of the present owner/managers of a bought business in order for the profits to grow. Therefore the earn-out is a common method in the purchase of people businesses. It tends to avoid, from the purchaser's point of view, the problem of a business which is highly dependent on a skilled individual being torpedoed shortly after being taken over because that individual walks away from the business. In contrast an earn-out is not suitable in cases where the seller – who is to receive the additional payment – is not prepared to remain in the business in the future.

In the case of earn-outs it is important that the original business is kept separate from other businesses that may be owned by the purchaser. This enables performance to be clearly identified in order to assess the size of the future payments. In reality unless the earn-out is over a short period of, say, one year, a purchaser is likely to want to make alterations to the business he has bought before the earn-out has run its course. If that is the case, then the seller should not agree to such changes unless his own position as regards the future payments is safeguarded. This type of situation gives rise to a large number of disputes and though there have been earn-outs over periods up to at least five years, it is best for a seller to limit the period to one to two years if possible.

Whether or not the seller is prepared to accept an earn-out depends on his objectives in selling in the first place. It has to be remembered that if the business does not perform, even if it is kept separate from the purchaser's other businesses, then the seller will not receive the additional payments. Being conscious of this should make a seller extremely wary when negotiating the terms of any earn-out.

Alternative cash payments

There are a number of ways of making cash payments to ensure that the price requirement of the seller is obtained. One of these, the placement of shares by the seller so that they are converted into cash, has already been mentioned. Others have been mentioned in Chapter 5 since they can give rise to various tax structuring benefits.

To summarise, there are three main ways that should be considered in negotiating method of payment.

First there are additional pension payments paid by the company into a special pension fund to provide a pension to the current owner–managers. This of course is not a payment method that can be used for a shareholder who is not actually employed in the business.

The second is for a dividend payment to be made by the company being sold. There are constraints upon a company's ability to pay dividends and these will have to be taken into account before deciding that this is a suitable course of action. In both these instances such payments reduce the asset value of the company being sold and therefore the purchaser will adjust the price that he is prepared to pay for the business. Overall, however, the seller is still receiving the required consideration.

A third possibility is for the seller, assuming he has been involved in the management of the company, to retain an employment or a consultancy contract with the company.

All three of these methods have significant tax implications depending upon the exact circumstances of the transaction.

Heads of Agreement

A Heads of Agreement is a document or letter which sets out the main areas of agreement between the seller and the purchaser. It will state, among other things, what is being sold, the price which is payable, the method and timing of payment and the conditions that must be fulfilled prior to completion by either the purchaser or the seller so that the sale can take place. Inevitably, the document will state that the agreement reached is subject to agreeing the final contractual terms. Thus a Heads of Agreement is not a binding sale contract.

The timing of signing Heads of Agreement can vary widely. Views as to when they should be signed are various but in reality the timing depends more upon the nature and the speed with which a transaction is taking place than anything else. A Heads of Agreement can, in principle, be a simple exchange of letters setting out the basic terms. If that is the route taken, then a lot of detailed negotiations must be anticipated between the signing of Heads of Agreement and the signing of a contract. Alternatively, the seller can effectively try to negotiate all the detail before signing Heads of Agreement. This will take much longer but should enable contracts to be drawn up and signed much more quickly. From the seller's point of view the latter does mean that he could, if he wished, continue negotiating with other parties without feeling that he was acting in bad faith. However, a long delay in reaching Heads of Agreement can cause a potential buyer who is negotiating strongly to become concerned about whether the seller is serious or is in fact negotiating with some other parties. It has certainly been known for potential purchasers to be upset by long delays in signing Heads of Agreement and withdraw from the transaction. On balance, for the smaller business a fairly early signing of Heads of Agreement in comparatively simple terms is the recommended route. But this has to be balanced against the potential difficulty of resuscitating negotiations with other parties should the preferred buyer fall out. The longer the gap from previous negotiations the more difficult it is to resuscitate them satisfactorily.

Once Heads of Agreement are signed the purchaser will expect that negotiations with other parties will cease. However, as already mentioned it is important to keep other parties interested as best one can in case the preferred deal falls through. It is certainly worth finding out how keen they would be to reopen negotiations should the first choice purchaser not proceed. It is surprising how often it is possible to keep a back-up buyer on the edge of the arena.

After Heads of Agreement are signed it might be thought that negotiations proceed in an orderly and calm way. That is rarely so. In one case some years ago Heads of Agreement were signed fairly late in negotiations after most of the differences had been ironed out. The buyer showed extreme keenness and pushed for early exchange of contracts. After some lengthy late-night negotiations the meeting for the signing and exchange of contracts was finally set up. You can imagine the consternation when right at the beginning of that meeting the chairman of the purchasing company declared that he wanted a 10 per cent reduction in the price before proceeding any further. There was no reason stated and it appeared that his negotiating stance was a belief that the seller had gone so far down the path that he could not now withdraw. After seven hours of discussions a compromise reduction of 5 per cent was agreed. What the purchaser never knew was that his negotiating position for a reduction at that late stage was extremely strong. The next highest price that had been offered was less than 40 per cent of the price he was paying. The seller and his advisers had rather frayed nerves by the time contracts were signed.

Due diligence

Due diligence refers to the overall process whereby a purchaser satisfies himself that making the purchase is a sensible move on his part and that what he is being told he is buying he is in fact buying. In reality the due diligence process commences once a purchaser shows interest in buying. Throughout negotiations the purchaser will be enhancing his knowledge of the business from whatever source is available. Once negotiations are seriously under way then the purchaser will probably require that certain specialists visit the business to make various assessments. Depending on how the negotiations are proceeding these will normally take place after Heads of Agreement have been signed.

The two most usual investigations will be by a valuer in respect of properties and by accountants in respect of the company's financial records. But there could be investigations by other specialists depending upon the nature of the business. In addition there will be the legal 'due diligence' whereby the purchaser's lawyers will be checking that the legal affairs of the business being purchased are in order. This will relate to such matters as the ownership of property and other assets, compliance with various statutory regulations, and the validity of significant agreements entered into by the business which are important to the purchaser.

The accountants' investigation will normally be wide ranging. It will not be an audit of the past history of the business but a report on that past history and how the information has been arrived at. They almost certainly will look at the budgeting performance of management, comparing previous budgets with what was actually achieved. This will help them to determine whether any forecasts that have been made by the seller during the negotiations are realistic, in the light of the past record. Among many other matters, they will be looking to check business trends for the various parts of the business, particularly sales, overheads and profits. They will be interested in the stock valuation if the value of stock held is material to the business. They will also check out the quality of the accounting systems in the business.

If anything negative is found during the course of the due diligence process this will be used by the buyer in an attempt to reduce the price. This is similar to what happens when a house-buyer receives a surveyor's report which shows some faults, whether significant or not, in the structure of the house he is buying. When told about any weaknesses the seller has a number of ways of reacting. How he approaches it will depend on his assessment of how serious he believes the weakness is in the eyes of the buyer. Some concerns will undoubtedly be overcome by showing the buyer that the particular weakness does not really exist or that it is totally immaterial to the ongoing success of the business. In the case of others he may have to accept a reduced price. In particular this would be the case if the agreed price was related to the net assets of the business but it was found that the assets were not in fact worth as much as the seller claimed.

Many of the more significant concerns can be dealt with by a combination of price adjustment and undertakings given within the contractual terms of the sale. However, in the worst cases, due diligence may uncover circumstances that the purchaser considers so important as to make him wish to withdraw from the transaction. Sometimes that will be exactly what does happen but on other occasions it is worth the seller's while to assess whether the purchaser's view of the situation is primarily a matter of perception or a real problem. If the former, the seller should attempt to alter the purchaser's perception so that the sale can proceed. If that is not possible the seller must decide whether other potential purchasers will react in a similar fashion. If they are likely to, then the problem is real and not just perceived, in which case the seller may have to reassess his own walk-away price, if he is keen to sell. If the problem has been uncovered by one potential buyer it will probably be uncovered by others. In any event the seller must not issue misleading information. If it is not disclosed at the time of sale nor uncovered by the purchaser during the due liligence process, it could give rise to claim from the purchaser at some future date. It is therefore well worthwhile for the seller to monitor the due diligence process so as to catch any potential problems at an early stage. This gives time to solve them if solved they can be.

Sale and purchase agreement

The sale and purchase agreement is the document which sets out the contractual terms on which the business is being sold by the seller and bought by the purchaser. The document will go into great detail specifying who the agreement is between, what the purpose of the agreement is, what is being sold, the price at which the transaction is taking place, the method of payment and when payment is to be made. Within the document there will almost inevitably be a section which sets down the essence of certain statements made during the course of negotiations by the seller and on which the purchaser is relying in making his purchase. These *warranties* are an integral part of the sale and purchase agreement. There will also be another section whereby the seller will undertake to indemnify the purchaser against certain specified losses if they should occur subsequent to the sale. Though this is not a legal guide on the selling of a business, it is as well for any seller to understand what warranties and indemnities are.

When a seller warrants something in a sale and purchase agreement he is making a legally binding statement in the knowledge that the buyer is relying on it. If it should prove to be incorrect then the seller will be under an obligation to the purchaser to make such payment to him as to recompense any loss. For example, a seller will probably have to warrant that he, or the company he is selling, is the owner of the plant that is included in the sale. If it should prove that one of the pieces of plant was not so owned, but perhaps subject to a hire purchase agreement, the buyer could claim recompense from the seller, probably for the amount of the outstanding payments that would have to be made to the hire purchase company.

A seller can protect himself from this risk by making specific disclosures to the purchaser prior to sale. In the above case, if there was a general warranty within the sale and purchase agreement that all the plant listed in the plant register belonged to the company, a disclosure could be made that there was one item that was in fact on hire purchase where ownership would not pass to the company until the final instalment had been paid. The purchaser could then negotiate what, if any, adjustment to the price he required before proceeding to completion of the transaction.

A purchaser might require an *indemnity* to be included in the sale and purchase agreement where there is an outstanding claim against the company being sold which cannot be quantified. It could be that the seller is quite certain that the claim will not result in any payment having to be made. A purchaser who is unlikely to know the full details of the case, may not be prepared to take that risk. He will therefore require an indemnity from the seller that if the company does in fact have to make payments in respect of such a claim the seller will reimburse the amount involved. In practice if this was a significant risk a purchaser would probably require that part of the sales proceeds be placed in a special account so that they were available to meet any claim arising.

In general a purchaser is going to require warranties from the seller about the following matters:

- certain information that has been provided during the course of negotiations. This may include the contents of an information document provided to the purchasers. In some cases a purchaser may even require that a seller warrants the factual statements contained within an accountant's report prepared for the purchaser during the course of due diligence. This should be resisted since the instructions for the report come from the purchaser and the control of their activities is with the purchaser. It is far safer to require the purchaser to set out the specific facts that he wants warranted rather than warrant that the document as a whole is correct;

- the financial position of the business. In particular, this is likely to contain warranties as to the value of assets and liabilities of the company and the past profitability of the business. If the business is being sold partly as a result of significant growth projections prepared by the seller then a purchaser is likely to seek warranties in respect of these. This is why when preparing a sales memorandum a seller should avoid making such projections. This is particularly important when the seller is not going to have any control over the business once the sale has taken place;

- the ownership of assets;
- the tax situation of the business. This is a complex area since all sales and purchases of business involve material taxation implications. The warranties will not merely require a statement that the company has met all its tax liabilities to date but also that it has not carried out any transactions which are likely to have tax implications for the future. Any seller needs to have good professional advice to deal with this point.

Other agreements

Depending on the nature of the business which is being sold and its circumstances there may be a series of additional agreements that need to be agreed and signed at the same time as a sale and purchase agreement. For instance if the seller is continuing within the business for some time after the sale it may be necessary for a service agreement to be drawn up setting out the terms of employment. This will also be the case if there is to be some form of consultancy agreement with the seller. There may be a need for assignments of leases, particularly where either the business being sold is not a limited company or where the properties used by the company are leased to the selling shareholder rather than direct to the company. There will also be a requirement for a lease agreement if the company being sold occupies a freehold property that is to remain within the ownership of the selling shareholder.

Exchange of contracts

Finally, when all has been agreed and set down in the various documents that are required the point has arrived at which the sale can be made contractually binding on both the purchaser and the seller. This is achieved by signing the contracts and exchanging the signed copies between the two parties. Then, and only then, will the contract become binding.

In some cases the above process takes place on the same day as actual completion. However, this will only happen when there are no conditions within the contract that have to be fulfilled between exchange of contracts and completion which require time to satisfy. If time is required the contract will state quite specifically when the completion will be. That is when the price will be paid, assuming that is what is set down in the contract.

10   *After The Sale*

On the morning after completion of the sale the seller wakes up with a great sense of relief. It is all over. He has his money and has achieved the objectives he set himself when he decided to sell the business. The late-night signing meeting and the bottles of champagne afterwards are now but a memory. Payment is on the way to the bank and all he has to do is to pay the advisers' bills before settling down to reap the benefit of his achievements. It's done. It's over. But is it?

Claims

It is almost impossible to be completely sure that it is really all over. Even where payment is by cash, drawn on a bank, payable at completion, with no follow on payments and no future involvement in the business, there can still be repercussions. Fortunately if the seller has been well advised and has disclosed all he should to the purchaser then the risks of future involvement are minimal. However, if something of substance should arise subsequent to completion, which enables the purchaser to make a claim against the seller, that is indeed what will probably happen. Once again the seller will be involved. After all it is he who has made statements and agreed the contractual terms on which the purchaser is entitled to rely should he have a need.

Fortunately, in most cases, that does not happen. So generally the seller can set about using the proceeds of the sale for the purposes which he originally intended. In many cases, particularly where a sizeable sum of money is involved sound advice on future investments should be sought from the various professionals who are available to help. Having gone to such great lengths, first to build up a business with significant value and then to go through the process of selling it, it makes sense to take steps to protect what has been gained.

Deferred payments

If part of the consideration has been deferred, the seller will have a significant ongoing interest in the business. Whether this is from inside the business or from outside will depend on the terms that have been agreed. What is important is that the seller monitors what is happening. He will then be prepared to take defensive measures should anything occur which could mean that he will not be paid out according to plan. These are not always easy to spot, but it is important to keep close to the decision makers in the purchasing business. Naturally this will be considerably easier if, as part of the transaction, the seller is continuing to work in the business. If for some reason the performance of the business starts to deteriorate, either as a result of its own activities or because of the activities of the new owners, the seller should attempt to bring forward the deferred payments as quickly as possible. This may mean renegotiating that part of the transaction in order to obtain a cash receipt up front rather than the deferred payment. It is wrong to assume that just because the contract says payment will be made on a particular date, the purchaser will, in fact, be in a position to make such a payment. So the message is to keep in touch.

Earn-outs

If the transaction has involved an earn-out involvement by the seller after formal completion is likely to be high. As part of such an earn-out the seller will almost certainly have entered into certain obligations regarding his future involvement in the business and it is important that he carries them out. This will avoid providing the purchaser with grounds for non-payment of future amounts due. Being involved in this way gives the seller much greater ability to monitor what is happening. Indeed, in many earn-outs, the seller will maintain considerable control over the destiny of the business. As mentioned in Chapter 9, this is the principal way the seller can be sure that the business is continuing in a similar form as before, so that payments due on the earn-out are more readily calculated.

However, business life does not stand still. In many cases the purchaser will require changes at some point during the earn-out period. Clearly if the business is doing badly then the purchaser would be unwise to leave things alone. The extent to which a seller in this situation is able to negotiate the reworking of the earn-out in his favour will depend on the particular circumstances.

It is not only because businesses get into difficulties after being taken over that earn-out arrangements have to be changed. It is possible that the purchaser will buy yet another business which he wishes to combine with the one that he has already bought. This provides the original seller with an ideal opportunity to negotiate a way out of the earn-out on terms favourable to himself. The purchaser will be keen to initiate changes to make the most of his second purchase and is not likely to be happy to see such changes balked because of an outstanding financial arrangement. Despite the fact that the cards might seem to be stacked in favour of the original purchaser, in reality, this has not generally proved to be the case, assuming the original business is still performing well.

Leases

Apart from involvement in the business after completion, there are one or two situations which could still boomerang on to the seller. One is in the case of leases. If the seller held leases in his own name, which were then assigned at the time of the sale to the purchaser, he will, of course, remain responsible to the landlord for those leases should the purchaser fail to meet the obligations of the lease. Such obligations may not only be in respect of rent but also repairs and maintenance. From a seller's point of view it may be better to arrange for a new lease to be issued by the landlord to the purchaser, rather than assigning an existing lease. Whether this is worth the effort will depend on the seller's assessment of the creditworthiness of the purchaser. It will also depend to a significant extent on the length of the lease outstanding at the time of sale.

Guarantees

Another area of continuing concern will be in respect of guarantees. When building up a business it is not unusual for the owners to give various personal guarantees to support the activities of the business. The most obvious of these, as previously mentioned, is to guarantee a bank in support of borrowings, but guarantees may also have been given in respect of leases, hire-purchase agreements, performance bonds and similar arrangements. When selling a business it may not always be possible for the seller to extract himself from all of these as part of the sale. It is important therefore when assessing whether to proceed with the transaction to be quite clear what ongoing risks there are, however unreal the risk may appear at the time.

If an owner has gone about the sale of his business in a structured manner, obtained good advice and understood the negotiating process, the odds are that he will have achieved nearly all, if not all, the objectives which were originally set out when deciding to sell. And he will retain peace of mind.

Appendices

1 *Ten Major Issues on Sale of a Business*

1. Defining the objectives to be achieved for the owners.

2. Setting realistic price expectations.

3. Having sufficient time to maximise value.

4. Maintaining confidentiality.

5. Comparing offers received.

6. Maintaining interest of a 'reserve' buyer.

7. Assessing effect of changes to offer during negotiations.

8. Maximising the tax benefits.

9. Ensuring the business continues to run smoothly during negotiations.

10. Stamina.

2 Seller's Checklist

Reasons for sale

1. Are you selling:
   - to retire?
   - because of ill-health?
   - because other owners wish to?
   - to go and do something else?
   - because you have to raise money?
   - because of some other reason?

2. Are you being honest with yourself?

Objectives of sale

3. Have you defined your objectives?

4. Do you want a quick sale?

5. Do you want cash now? All or part?

6. Do you want a continuing role after the sale?

Alternatives

7. Are there alternatives to an outright sale?
   - partial sale of whole?
   - splitting and selling part?
   - flotation?
   - sale and leaseback of assets?
   - share buy-in?
   - payment of exceptional dividend?

Timing of sale

8. (a) Is it a forced sale?
   (b) If so, how quickly is the money needed?

9.   Is the economic cycle beneficial?

10.   Is the industry cycle beneficial?

11.   How long will be needed to maximise profits?

12.   Does the reason for sale dictate the timing of the sale?

What is for sale

13.   Is it an asset or company sale?

14.   Is it an asset-based or people-based business?

15.   Will a third party (eg a franchisor) have a particular influence on the sale?

Key factors

16.   Which are likely to be the key factors to a potential purchaser:

- profits?
- assets?
- growth rate?
- location?
- customer base?
- supplier?
- catchment potential?
- market position?
- technology?
- some other?

Professional advisers

17.   Which professional adviser will be needed:

- lawyer?
- accountant?
- tax adviser?
- valuer?
- patent agent?
- actuary?
- business transfer agent?
- merger and acquisition boutique?
- merchant bank?

18. What fees will be payable to each if:
    - a sale takes place?
    - a sale does not take place?

19. When will fees be payable?

20. Are the fee terms clearly set out in each engagement letter?

Preparation for sale

21. Can profit improvement be achieved?

22. Is there discretionary expenditure which can be eliminated?
    - travel?
    - entertainment?
    - family employment costs?
    - excess directors' remuneration?
    - motor expenses?
    - overseas properties?
    - aircraft or helicopter?
    - sponsorship?

23. Should stock or debtor provisioning policy be revised?

24. Can borrowing be reduced by:
    - reducing stock levels?
    - collecting debts more quickly?
    - paying creditors later?

25. Is the condition of the fixed assets satisfactory?

26. Do the premises give a good first impression?

27. Should leases be renegotiated?

28. Are there surplus assets to be sold to reduce borrowings?

29. Have all business assets been clearly identified?

30. Is there more than one business? Should they be separated?

31. Are key employees tied in?

32. When should the various groups be told about the intention to sell?

33. Should terms with customers or suppliers be renegotiated?

34. (a) Will knowledge of sale affect relationship with employees, customers or suppliers?
     (b) If so, how can negative effects be overcome?

Taxation

35. Have you a good knowledgeable tax adviser?

36. Do you intend to emigrate?

37. For tax purposes, is it preferable to receive proceeds as income or capital?

38. How will the allocation of values between assets affect the tax liability?

39. (a) Was the business trading on 31 March 1982?
     (b) If so, has a valuation as of that date been carried out?

40. Can you claim retirement relief?

41. Can you claim roll-over relief?

42. (a) Are there trading losses?
     (b) If so, can they be off-set against capital gains?
     (c) Will they be available for off-set to a purchaser?

43. Have the tax consequences of deferred consideration been considered?

44. To avoid payment of VAT, will the sale comply with Transfer of Undertaking Regulations?

45. Has your inheritance tax situation both before and after the sale been considered?

Price

46. What is the estimated value of the business?

47. Will a purchaser value on the basis of profits, assets or entry cost?

48. Are there exceptional features which warrant a premium price?

49. Have you set your target price?

50. Have you set your walk-away price?

51. Can you avoid disclosing your asking price in the early stage of negotiations?

Sales Memorandum

52. Who will prepare the sales memorandum?

53. Does it contain a brief description of:

- the nature of the business?
- customers?
- suppliers?
- ownership?
- legal structure?
- reason for sale?
- management and employees?
- significant assets?

54. Does it contain:

- a financial summary (2+ years)?
- a review of balance sheets?
- a summary of prospects (not forecasts)?
- a timetable for replies?

55. Is the memorandum misleading?

56. Does the memorandum comply with the Financial Services Act?

57. Is the memorandum being issued as prescribed by the Financial Services Act?

Finding a buyer

58. Have you identified the characteristics of the most likely buyer?

59. Are there potential buyers?

- known to you?
- known to your advisers?
- among your suppliers?
- among your customers?

60. Should other potential buyers be identified by:

- research?
- advertising?

61.   Should buyers be sought from overseas?

62.   Are there known new entrants to the industry?

63.   Could there be identifiable wild cards?

64.   Are you prepared to sell to existing management? Will they want to buy?

65.   Have you identified individuals with whom to make initial contact?

66.   If writing a letter, have you prepared standard wording?

67.   Do your initial approaches fall within the law (Financial Services Act)?

68.   If advertising, can you identify those responses most likely to be serious?

69.   Are they principals?

70.   Have you prepared your standard confidentiality agreement?

71.   Before sending out the Sales Memorandum have you ensured you have received a signed confidentiality agreement?

72.   If you have many interested parties, should you seek indicative offers at an early stage?

Negotiations

73.   Do you have sufficient knowledge of indicative offers to reduce negotiations to a small short list of potential buyers?

74.   Do you need to revise your target or walk-away prices in view of indicative offers?

75.   Have you provided adequate information to obtain best offers?

76.   Are you satisfied bidders can pay?

77.   Are the buyer's proposed conditions acceptable?

78.   Can you identify a preferred buyer?

79.   Can you keep the interest of some other potential buyers as back-up?

Methods of payment

80. Are you prepared to accept the proposed method of payment:

    - cash now?
    - shares in a large quoted company?
    - shares in a small quoted company?
    - shares in a private company?
    - cash, partly in the future?

81. Are future payments secured or guaranteed?

82. How dependent on performance are future payments?

83. Have tax efficient payment methods been considered?

    - pensions?
    - dividends?
    - consultancy?
    - future employment?

Heads of Agreement

84. Should you sign at an early or late stage?

85. Have major issues been agreed?

Due diligence

86. Have you kept close to the due diligence process?

87. Can you counter concerns that the process raises for the buyer?

88. (a) Are the issues raised of major concern?
    (b) If so, should you reduce your price expectation?
    (c) Or do you withdraw to give time to remedy the concern and return another time?

Sale and purchase agreement

89. Do you have an experienced lawyer?

90. Can you limit the warranties you give?

91. (a) Do you understand what you are signing?
    (b) All of it?

92.   Are you sure you are getting what you want to achieve?

After the sale

93.   Should you maintain ongoing interest in the activities of the business to protect the future payments to you?

94.   Can you insure against residual claims arising from warranties given or latent liabilities in respect of assigned leases, and similar agreements?

95.   Can you now sit back and be content?

Index